Group
Loveland, Colorado

Treasure Hunt Bible Adventure Director Manual
Copyright © 1999 Group Publishing, Inc.

All rights reserved. No part of this book may be reproduced in any manner whatsoever without prior written permission from the publisher, except where noted on handouts and in the case of brief quotations embodied in critical articles and reviews. For information, write Permissions, Group Publishing, Inc., Dept. PD, P.O. Box 481, Loveland, CO 80539.

Unless otherwise noted, Scripture taken from the HOLY BIBLE, NEW INTERNATIONAL VERSION®. Copyright © 1973, 1978, 1984 by International Bible Society. Used by permission of Zondervan Publishing House. All rights reserved.

Credits
Treasure Hunt Bible Adventure Coordinator: Jody Brolsma
Chief Creative Officer: Joani Schultz
Copy Editor: Helen Turnbull
Art Director: Kari K. Monson
Cover Art Director: Lisa Chandler
Cover Photographer: Craig DeMartino
Cover Designers: Becky Hawley and Jerry Krutar
Illustrators: Amy Bryant and Drew Rose
Rain Forest Art: Pat Allen
Rain Forest Art Photographer: Linda Bohm
Production Manager: Peggy Naylor

ISBN 0-7644-9909-2
Printed in the United States of America.
10 9 8 7 6 5 4 3 2 1   00 99

CONTENTS

GET READY FOR THE ADVENTURE OF A LIFETIME!
An Introduction to Treasure Hunt Bible Adventure 7
- Welcome to Treasure Hunt Bible Adventure! 9
- The Overview 10
- Inspecting Your Treasure Hunt Bible Adventure Starter Kit 12

TREASURE HUNT BIBLE ADVENTURE BASICS
What You'll Want to Know Before You Go Exploring 15
- Why Treasure Hunt Bible Adventure? 17
- How Will Kids Learn the Bible? 19
- What's a Discovery Site? 22
- What's a Clue Crew? 23
- Who's Who on the Crew? 26
- Where Do Middle Schoolers Fit In? 27
- Do Teenagers Have a Role at Treasure Hunt Bible Adventure? 28
- What's a Student Book? 29
- Who Is Chadder Chipmunk™? 30
- Can Kids *Really* Make Their Own Snacks? 31

OPERATION KID-TO-KID™
Sharing the Treasure of Jesus 33
- What Is Operation Kid-to-Kid™? 35
- Planning for Operation Kid-to-Kid™ 37
- Operation Kid-to-Kid™ News Release 39

MAPPING OUT YOUR TREASURE HUNT BIBLE ADVENTURE
How to Create a Radical Rain Forest 41
- Planning Calendar 43
- When and Where to Begin Your Treasure Hunt 53
- Facilities: Turn Your Church Into a Tropical Rain Forest 56

Contents

Supplies: Everything You Need for an Exciting Expedition..........................59
Bonus Idea!..69
Daily Supplies..70
Daily Schedules...72

RECRUITMENT
Calling All Adventurers! 81
Recruiting Discovery Site Leaders 83
Treasure Hunt Sing & Play Leader..85
Craft Cave Leader..86
Jungle Gym Games Leader...87
Treasure Treats Leader..88
Bible Exploration Leader..89
Chadder's Treasure Hunt Theater Leader..................................90
Treasure Time Finale Leader...91
Preschool Bible Treasure Land Director......................................92
Enlisting Clue Crew Leaders...93
Enlisting Clue Crew Leaders for Preschoolers...........................95
Enlisting Treasure Hunt Sign-In Personnel and Registrar..........97
Enlisting a Treasure Hunt Bible Adventure Photographer..........98
Filling Out Your Staff...99

LEADER TRAINING
Preparing Your Staff for an Amazing Adventure! 101
Using the *Discover!* Video..103
"Gearing Up for the Adventure!" Leader Training Meeting.......104
For Clue Crew Leaders Only...113
For Clue Crew Leaders of Preschoolers Only..........................117

PUBLICITY
Getting Your Church and Community "Clued In"........119
Promoting Treasure Hunt Bible Adventure
  in Your Church and Community..121
Treasure Hunt Bible Adventure Clip Art....................................124
Treasure Hunt Bible Adventure Bulletin Inserts.......................125
Treasure Hunt Bible Adventure Table Tent...............................126
Invitation to Parents...127
News Release..128
Community Flier...129
Publicity Skit...130

REGISTRATION
Welcoming Your Explorers 133
- Making an Unforgettable Impression 135
- Setting Up Clue Crews 137
- Let Clue Crew Leaders Help With Treasure Hunt Sign-In 140
- Registration Day Is Here! 141
- Registration: Here They Come! 143
- After Registration 144
- Treasure Hunt Bible Adventure Registration Instructions 145
- Age-Level Roster 147
- Clue Crew Roster 148
- Alphabetical Master List 149
- Treasure Hunt Bible Adventure Registration Form 150

CLUES FOR YOU!
Tips for a Terrific Treasure Hunt! 151
- Daily Staff Devotions 153
- Bells and Whistles 158
- Taking Home the Treasure 159
- Health and Safety Concerns 163
- Kids With Special Needs 165
- Welcoming Newcomers 166
- Responsibility: Let 'Em Have It! 167

ENDING THE EXPEDITION
Closing Program and Follow-Up Ideas 169
- Helping Children Know Jesus 171
- You've Found the Treasure! 172
- Closing Program: Taking the Treasure Home 172
- Follow-Up Ideas 174
- "You're a Gem!" Certificate for Staff 176
- "You're a Gem!" Certificate for Children 177
- Staff Appreciation Bulletin 178
- Evaluating Your Treasure Hunt Bible Adventure Program 179
- Discovery Site Leader VBS Evaluation 180
- Clue Crew Leader VBS Evaluation 181
- Treasure Hunt Bible Adventure Evaluation 183

INDEX 185

GET READY FOR THE ADVENTURE OF A LIFETIME!

An Introduction to

Treasure Hunt Bible Adventure

Welcome to TREASURE HUNT BIBLE ADVENTURE!

X marks the spot...for VBS excitement! Grab your compass, dust off your binoculars, and be sure your flashlight has batteries. You're hot on the trail to Treasure Hunt Bible Adventure, where kids discover Jesus—the greatest treasure of all. Treasure Hunt Bible Adventure is an exciting, fun-filled, Bible-based program your kids will love. (We know because we tested everything in a field test last summer. Look for our Field Test Findings to learn what we discovered and how that will make your program the best!) Your teachers will love Treasure Hunt Bible Adventure, too, because it's so easy to prepare for! And *you'll* love it because kids will explore how the Bible maps the way to amazing riches, showing us the way to trust, love, pray, live, and know Jesus—the greatest treasure of all!

Kids start off each day by forming small groups called Clue Crews. All the Clue Crews gather at Treasure Hunt Sing & Play to do fun motions to upbeat Bible songs that introduce kids to the concepts they'll be learning that day. Then Clue Crews "trek" to five different Discovery Sites. They meet Chadder Chipmunk™ on video, "monkey around" at Jungle Gym Games, sample "vine" dining at Treasure Treats, explore the excitement and drama of Bible adventures, and create cool treasure in the Craft Cave. Then crews gather to participate in each day's Treasure Time Finale. And throughout the week, children work on a treasure they'll share during Operation Kid-to-Kid™. This missions project allows the kids at your church to impact children around the globe!

Preschoolers have a special program of their own. They join the older kids for opening and closing activities, and in between they enjoy fun, age-appropriate, Bible-learning activities in the Preschool Bible Treasure Land. There, preschoolers hear a Bible story, then explore the story with all five senses through Rain Forest Exploration Stations. Later, children continue their discoveries and work off some energy during Jungle Gym Playtime. They also meet Chadder Chipmunk and enjoy Treasure Treats made by the older kids.

This Director Manual is your guide to mapping out a successful adventure. It contains everything you need to plan a successful program, recruit and train volunteers, publicize your program, and follow up with kids and their families after Treasure Hunt Bible Adventure. **The adventure has begun! Get ready to guide your kids to the greatest treasure of all—Jesus!**

A CLUE FOR YOU!
Make this Director Manual even easier to use! Cut away the binding, then use a three-hole punch to make holes near the spine. Place the pages in a three-ring binder, with divider pages separating each section.

A CLUE FOR YOU!
As Treasure Hunt Director, you'll want to know what's happening each day. Refer to the "Treasure Hunt Bible Adventure Overview Chart" on pages 10-11 to get an overview of the Bible stories and biblical truths elementary kids cover. You'll discover how these truths are reinforced creatively throughout each day.

TREASURE HUNT BIBLE ADVENTURE OVERVIEW

This is what everyone else is doing! At Treasure Hunt Bible Adventure, the daily Bible Point is carefully integrated into each Discovery Site activity to reinforce Bible learning. Each Discovery Site is an important part of kids' overall learning experience.

	BIBLE POINT	BIBLE STORY	BIBLE VERSE	TREASURE HUNT SING & PLAY	CRAFT CAVE	JUNGLE GYM GAMES
DAY 1	The Bible shows us the way to trust.	Peter walks to Jesus on the Sea of Galilee (Matthew 14:22-33).	"Do not let your hearts be troubled. Trust in God" (John 14:1a).	• He's Got the Whole World in His Hands • The B-I-B-L-E • Where Do I Go? • I've Found Me a Treasure (chorus and verse 1)	**Craft** Jungle Gel **Application** Kids need to trust the Craft Cave Leader that Jungle Gel really works. In the same way, we need to trust God when things in life seem impossible.	**Games** • Swamp Squish • Peter's Windy Walk • The River Bend • Treasure Tag • Pass-Along Peter **Application** The Bible teaches us that God is powerful and that we can trust him.
DAY 2	The Bible shows us the way to love.	Jesus washes the disciples' feet (John 13:1-17).	"A new command I give you: Love one another" (John 13:34a).	• Put a Little Love in Your Heart • I've Found Me a Treasure (add verse 2) • Jesus Loves Me	**Craft** Operation Kid-to-Kid Magnetic Bible Bookmarks **Application** Just as the magnet links the two children on the bookmark together, the Bible connects us with others around the world.	**Games** • Monkeys Love Bananas • Footrace • Gold Coin Keep-Away • Firefly Fling • Mosquito Net **Application** As the Bible shows us how to love, we can love others.
DAY 3	The Bible shows us the way to pray.	Jesus prays for his disciples and all believers, and then he is arrested (John 17:1–18:11).	"I pray also for those who will believe in me through their message, that all of them may be one" (John 17:20a-21b).	• Let Us Pray • Hey Now • I've Found Me a Treasure (add verse 3)	**Craft** Surprise Treasure Chests **Application** When kids open the treasure chest, they'll be surprised at the "riches" inside. When we open our hearts to God in prayer, we'll be surprised by his loving response.	**Games** • Savor the Flavor • Centipede Scurry • Message Mime • It's a Jungle! • Flowers of Blessing **Application** It's easy to talk to God.
DAY 4	The Bible shows us the way to Jesus.	Jesus is crucified, rises again, and appears to Mary Magdalene (John 19:1–20:18).	"For God so loved the world that he gave his one and only Son, that whoever believes in him shall not perish but have eternal life" (John 3:16).	• He's Alive • Make Your Home in My Heart • Good News • Oh, How I Love Jesus • I've Found Me a Treasure (add verse 4)	**Craft** Good News Treasure Pouches **Application** The colorful beads on the Treasure Pouch will remind kids of the good news that Jesus died for our sins and rose again!	**Games** • Roll Away the Stone • Butterfly Breakout • Manic Monarchs • Jungle-Bird Jiggle • He Has Risen! **Application** Our lives can be changed because Jesus rose from the dead.
DAY 5	The Bible shows us the way to live.	Paul stands firm in his faith, even in a shipwreck (Acts 27:1-44).	"If you love me, you will obey what I command" (John 14:15).	• The B-I-B-L-E • Got a Reason for Livin' Again • I've Found Me a Treasure (entire song)	**Craft** Rain Forest Creatures **Application** Kids add color and "life" to Rain Forest Creatures just as God's Word adds color and meaning to our lives.	**Games** • Man-Overboard Tag • Out to Sea • Snake Swap • Crash Course • Cargo Toss **Application** Even when life seems scary or difficult, we can have confidence that God is in control.

This overview chart shows you the entire program at a glance. Refer to the chart to see how each Discovery Site's activities supplement other activities to help kids discover Jesus.

TREASURE TREATS	CHADDER'S TREASURE HUNT THEATER	BIBLE EXPLORATION	TREASURE TIME FINALE
Snack Peter's Adventure Cakes **Application** Peter's adventure began when he trusted Jesus. Jesus wants us to trust him, too.	**Video Segment** Chadder and his friends begin searching for a hidden treasure. They stumble onto the deck of the SS Hope, where Wally the parrot warns them to watch out for Riverboat Bob. Chadder's afraid, so Ryan, the first mate, tells him to trust God. The kids go to Whistle Cave, followed by Ned and Pete, two scraggly sailors who want the treasure for themselves. The kids find the treasure map, moments before they're trapped by a cave-in! **Application** • Where do you turn when you're afraid? • How does the Bible help you trust in God? • Mark your Student Book at a Trust Verse.	**Peter Walks on Water** • Experience being in a ship during a storm. • Try walking on "water." • Discuss how Peter learned to trust Jesus.	• Watch how a pin can go into a balloon, without popping the balloon! • Use balloons to review the story of Peter walking on the water. • Receive gem treasures as reminders that we are precious to God.
Snack Love Chests **Application** Jesus showed love for his disciples when he washed their feet. Today's snack shows that love is a great treasure.	**Video Segment** Chadder sits in an old mine car, and the car takes off, racing through the cave. Near the cave exit stands Riverboat Bob. He hits the hand brake and Chadder goes flying, right into the boxes Ryan has been stacking on deck. Chadder thinks Ryan will be mad, but Ryan says he follows Jesus' example of showing love. Chadder leaves to look for his friends, but runs into Riverboat Bob instead! **Application** • Role play how you think Ryan will react to the mess Chadder made. • How can the Bible help you when it's hard to love someone? • How can the Love Verse you highlighted help you love this week?	**Jesus Washes the Disciples' Feet** • Go on a barefoot hunt to find the Upper Room. • Have their feet washed by their Clue Crew Leader. • Help wash their Clue Crew Leader's feet. • Help one another put their shoes back on.	• See how someone shows unexpected love to the Treasure Time Finale Leader. • Receive heart locks and keys as treasures to remind them that loving actions open people's hearts.
Snack Prayer Treasure Mix **Application** Jesus' prayer teaches us to pray. The items in the Prayer Treasure Mix remind kids to pray about specific things.	**Video Segment** Chadder awakes in the mine and finds Hayley and Tim. They find a clue and decide to ask Ryan for help. The kids find Ryan in prayer, and Ryan shows them the Bible story of Jesus praying. Chadder wanders off, and Colonel Mike sees him and mistakes him for a scoundrel. Colonel Mike tells Chadder to walk the plank. **Application** • Pray in your crew for the child who'll receive your Spanish Bible. • Is there ever a time when you shouldn't pray? Explain. • How can you pray as Jesus taught?	**Jesus Prays** • Learn ways to pray for themselves. • Practice praying for various groups of people. • Create a mural with their hand prints to represent Jesus' prayer for all believers.	• Watch a skit about what it might be like for God to listen to our prayers. • Receive magnifying glass treasures as reminders that prayer brings us closer to God.
Snack Empty Tombs **Application** On the third day, Jesus' tomb stood empty. These scrumptious snacks are empty, too.	**Video Segment** Ryan explains that Chadder's a friend, and Colonel Mike points the kids toward the monkey tree. Chadder loses the map, but Ryan assures him that Jesus is the real treasure. The wind blows the map back again, and the hunt continues. The kids find the treasure chest, and Chadder finds the key to the chest hidden in the old tree. Just as they open the chest, Ned and Pete step up to steal the treasure. **Application** • How do you get to heaven? • How can knowing the treasure of Jesus change your life? • Why is it important to know about the treasure of Jesus?	**Mary Magdalene at the Empty Tomb** • Experience the sadness of the crucifixion. • Hear Mary tell how she searched for her lost treasure—Jesus—at the empty tomb. • Hear "Jesus" call their names; then draw crosses on their mural hand prints to thank God for Jesus.	• Pray; then give their sins to "Jesus" and watch as he makes the sins disappear. • Receive personal messages from their Clue Crew Leaders that Jesus loves them. • Receive three gold coin treasures as reminders that Jesus is the most valuable treasure we have.
Snack Sailboat Sandwiches **Application** When Paul faced a shipwreck, his trust in God helped him. We can live an adventurous life when we believe in God.	**Video Segment** Ned and Pete plan to take the treasure, but Riverboat Bob steps in to help. Bob reveals that he's been watching over the kids all along. Colonel Mike wants to throw Ned and Pete to the alligators, but Ryan convinces him to show God's love. Hayley, Tim, and Chadder fantasize about what they'll do with the treasure, but decide to give the money to Colonel Mike to help him bring supplies and Bibles to people along the river. **Application** • How can the Bible help you make decisions this week? • What do you think about giving your Spanish Bible away? Why? • When are times you can use the Bible verses you marked this week?	**Paul Is Shipwrecked** • Be "handcuffed," and led inside a prisoner's ship. • Hear a fellow prisoner tell about Paul's experience in the ship. • Experience a shipwreck. • Discuss how Paul's life was in God's control.	• Use a "chirping parrot" to experience the importance of working together to tell others about Jesus. • Present their Spanish translations of the Gospel of John as a special offering. • Receive a compass as a reminder that the Bible gives us direction in life.

Inspecting Your TREASURE HUNT BIBLE ADVENTURE Starter Kit

Before you dig into your Treasure Hunt Bible Adventure program, inspect your Starter Kit to make sure it contains all the following items:

○ **Treasure Hunt Bible Adventure Director Manual (you're reading it now!)**—This is your guide to running Treasure Hunt Bible Adventure. It includes everything you need to plan, staff, and promote your church's best program ever! In it you'll find photocopiable handouts, letters, certificates, and more.

○ *Discover!* **video**—This video provides an overview of the entire Treasure Hunt Bible Adventure program. As you watch the video, you'll meet teachers and kids who've participated in Treasure Hunt Bible Adventure. You'll see for yourself how much fun Bible learning can be. The video also contains training material so you can feel confident that your staff is well prepared to run its very own Treasure Hunt Bible Adventure. Additionally, your Treasure Hunt Bible Adventure Director Manual tells you how to use this video as a quick promotional tool to get your church, kids, parents, and teachers excited about your program.

○ **Preschool Bible Treasure Land Director Manual**—This manual outlines five days of complete programs for children between the ages of three and five. The manual also contains supply lists, room setup and decoration ideas, exciting Bible-teaching ideas, and more to make your Preschool Bible Treasure Land *the* place to be!

○ **seven Discovery Site leader manuals:**
- **Treasure Hunt Sing & Play Leader Manual**
- **Treasure Treats Leader Manual**
- **Craft Cave Leader Manual**
- **Bible Exploration Leader Manual**
- **Chadder's Treasure Hunt Theater Leader Manual***
- **Jungle Gym Games Leader Manual**
- **Treasure Time Finale Leader Manual**

Each leader manual introduction contains detailed instructions for before, during, and after Treasure Hunt Bible Adventure, plus an overview of the entire program. Leader manuals include clear, step-by-step directions for each activity, guided discussion questions, valuable "A Clue for You!" tips, and "Field Test Findings" to make sure everything goes smoothly.

*Requires *Chadder's Treasure Hunt Adventure* video (available from Group Publishing, Inc., and your local Christian bookstore).

A CLUE FOR YOU!

Before you hand the leader manuals to your Discovery Site Leaders, be sure to skim the books to get an idea of what's happening in each area. You'll feel better prepared to answer questions that may arise.

○ ***Treasure Hunt Sing & Play* audiocassette**—This audiocassette provides Bible songs your kids will love, including the Treasure Hunt Bible Adventure theme song, "I've Found Me a Treasure." The cassette is recorded in split-track format so you can use just the accompaniment or add kids' voices. After you've listened to the cassette, give it to your Treasure Hunt Sing & Play Leader. He or she will use the cassette to teach kids the Treasure Hunt Bible Adventure songs. You may want to order additional cassettes so other leaders (especially those for Craft Cave, Treasure Treats, and Jungle Gym Games) can play the songs in the background as kids visit their Discovery Sites.

○ **Operation Kid-to-Kid brochure**—On Day 2, kids will learn about an exciting, meaningful missions project called Operation Kid-to-Kid. In Operation Kid-to-Kid, the children at your VBS will send Spanish-translations of the Gospel of John to Spanish-speaking children around the world! This brochure explains what Operation Kid-to-Kid is, how it was developed, who it will impact, and how the kids at your VBS will carry it out.

○ **Elementary Student Book**—There's no better book for kids to explore than God's Word! That's why kids at Treasure Hunt Bible Adventure will use the New International Version of the Gospel of John as their Student Books. During Treasure Hunt Bible Adventure, children will read, highlight, and create helpful tabs in their Bible books. Plus, each Student Book includes a Spanish translation of the Gospel of John. At the end of the week, kids will remove the Spanish Bible books to be sent to children in Spanish-speaking countries around the world!

○ **Preschool Student Book**—Preschoolers get to discover the treasure of God's Word in their own children's Bibles. Children will add stickers to the Bible pages, to help them remember the significance of each story. Preschool Student Books also include exciting activity pages for children to work on, plus ideas for family activities that will reinforce the Point at home. And, the Preschool Student Book contains a Spanish translation of the Gospel of John, so little ones can participate in Operation Kid-to-Kid.

○ **craft packet**—Use the thirteen items in this packet to create samples of all five Treasure Hunt Bible Adventure crafts. Kids will love these irresistible, engaging crafts, like Jungle Gel in its color-changing Gel Cell, Operation Kid-to-Kid Magnetic Bible Bookmarks, Surprise Treasure Chests (with an ear-catching surprise inside!), Good News Treasure Pouches, and cute Rain Forest Creatures. (Inside the packet, you'll find an informative flier that lists the enclosed items and shows what the finished crafts look like.)

○ **Decorating brochure**—Turn your church into a wild, tropical rain forest using the ideas from this brochure. You'll find easy decorating ideas for creating bridges, trees, animals, bugs, jungle huts, and much more!

○ **Geoami™**—Use this intriguing, "I-just-gotta-touch-it," "What-in-the-world-is that?" paper to create ancient-looking treasure maps. When you decorate a door, hallway, or bulletin board, Geoami adds the "cool factor."

○ **bag of sample items**—Add dazzle to your program with these "extras." In this bag you'll find publicity to help build excitement about your program, awards to recognize everyone's contribution, and souvenirs to leave a lasting impression.

If any Starter Kit items are missing or damaged, contact your local Christian bookstore for prompt replacement.

If you checked off everything on this list, you're ready to dig into your program.

May God bless you as you plan your TREASURE HUNT BIBLE ADVENTURE program!

TREASURE HUNT BIBLE ADVENTURE BASICS

What You'll Want to Know BEFORE YOU GO EXPLORING

Why TREASURE HUNT BIBLE ADVENTURE?

What makes Group's Treasure Hunt Bible Adventure different from other VBS programs?

● **At Treasure Hunt Bible Adventure, kids learn one important Bible Point each day.** Instead of trying to teach kids more than they can remember or apply, Treasure Hunt Bible Adventure focuses on one key biblical concept: **The Bible shows us the way.** This Bible Point is reinforced daily through Bible stories, Bible verses, and hands-on activities that help kids discover that the Bible is like a treasure map that leads us through life. Kids who attend your church regularly will enjoy discovering this important truth in fresh, new ways. And neighborhood kids who come to your VBS will hear the "meat" of the gospel right away. Each day kids will learn something new about how the Bible guides us.

Day 1: The Bible shows us the way to trust.
Day 2: The Bible shows us the way to love.
Day 3: The Bible shows us the way to pray.
Day 4: The Bible shows us the way to Jesus.
Day 5: The Bible shows us the way to live.

● **At Treasure Hunt Bible Adventure, kids learn the way they learn best.** Not all kids learn the same way, so Treasure Hunt Bible Adventure offers seven daily Discovery Sites to meet the needs of all kinds of learners. Each child will come away from each day remembering the Bible Point because kids will pick it up in a way that matches their learning style.

 Treasure Hunt Sing & Play's songs and motions will teach the Bible Point to your **musical learners.**

Jungle Gym Games, Bible Exploration, and Craft Cave allow **bodily-kinesthetic learners** to wiggle and move as they explore the Bible Point in active ways.

 Chadder's Treasure Hunt Theater lets **visual learners** discover the Bible Point through watching the *Chadder's Treasure Hunt Adventure* video.

Treasure Treats allows **interpersonal learners** the opportunity to explore what the Bible shows us as they make and serve snacks for the entire Treasure Hunt Bible Adventure.

Treasure Time Finale's dramatic and interactive programs help **linguistic learners** remember each day's Bible Point.

Every Discovery Site asks meaningful, thought-provoking questions that encourage **logical and introspective learners** to think about and apply the Bible Point.

● **At Treasure Hunt Bible Adventure, teachers teach the way they teach best.** Just like kids, teachers don't all think alike. Instead of forcing every teacher to teach the same material, Treasure Hunt Bible Adventure provides opportunities for you to enlist a variety of teachers. Got a great storyteller in your congregation? Recruit that person to lead Bible Exploration. Got a great athlete? Recruit that person to lead Jungle Gym Games. Because each Discovery Site is different, teachers can volunteer in their areas of expertise. And volunteers who are intimidated by the idea of teaching can join your staff as Clue Crew Leaders.

● **At Treasure Hunt Bible Adventure, no activity stands alone.** Instead of leading independent, isolated classes, Discovery Site Leaders see all the kids each day. Treasure Hunt Sing & Play songs play in the background during other activities. One of the crafts kids make during Craft Cave is given as an offering during Treasure Time Finale. The Jungle Gym Games Leader serves as an assistant Treasure Treats chef. The Bible Exploration Leader and the Treasure Time Finale Leader share supplies and volunteers. All Discovery Site Leaders assist in Treasure Time Finale. Each member of your Treasure Hunt Bible Adventure staff provides a unique and important part of kids' total VBS experience. With everyone working together, your staff will breeze through the week.

● **At Treasure Hunt Bible Adventure, kids take responsibility for what they're learning.** Throughout the week, kids travel to Discovery Sites with their Clue Crews—small groups of three to five kids. On the first day, each child chooses a job that he or she will do throughout the week. Kids may be Readers, Clue Keepers, Materials Managers, Cheerleaders, or Prayer People. From time to time, Discovery Site Leaders will call on kids to complete tasks that are part of their job descriptions.

Each Clue Crew also has an adult or teenage Clue Crew Leader. Clue Crew Leaders aren't teachers. They're simply part of Clue Crew families—like older brothers or sisters. Clue Crew Leaders participate in all the activities and encourage kids to talk about and apply what they're learning. Clue Crew Leaders who participated in Treasure Hunt Bible Adventure field tests saw kids encouraging other kids during the activities, helping younger crew members with difficult tasks, and reminding each other to use kind words. At Treasure Hunt Bible Adventure, kids put God's love into action!

● **At Treasure Hunt Bible Adventure, everyone is treated with respect.** Because kids travel in combined-age Clue Crews, big kids and little kids learn to work together. Instead of trying to compete with children their own age, older children help younger children during Craft Cave and Jungle Gym Games.

A Clue For You!

We've heard it again and again from VBS Directors everywhere: "This program brought out people's talents in wonderful new ways! People who never imagined that they could work with kids had a great time—and already volunteered to help next year!" So go for it! Look beyond "the usual" group of volunteers and bring in some new faces.

Younger children spark older children's imaginations during Bible Exploration and Treasure Time Finale.

Studies show that children learn as much—or more—when they're linked with kids of different ages. In fact, one study observed that children naturally chose to play with other children their age only 6 percent of the time. They played with children at least one year older or younger than them 55 percent of the time.

Think of Clue Crews as families in which kids naturally learn with and from one another. Social skills improve, self-esteem rises, cooperation increases, and discipline problems diminish.

Combined-age Clue Crews also allow people of any age (even entire families) to join you for your Treasure Hunt Bible Adventure program. You can even use combined-age Clue Crews to teach kids about being part of the body of Christ!

Knowing and understanding these distinctions will help you present Treasure Hunt Bible Adventure to your church or committee.

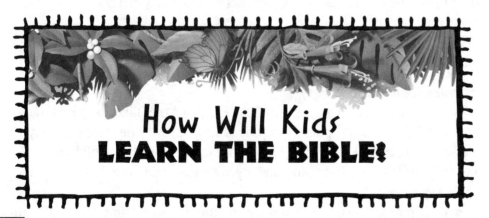

How Will Kids LEARN THE BIBLE?

Each day, kids will be exposed to a Bible Point as well as to a corresponding Bible story and verse. The chart on page 20 shows the Bible content kids will cover each day.

If you usually incorporate memory verses into your program, you can have kids memorize the daily Bible verses provided in this chart. Since children actually look

Field Test Findings

"The older kids at my church like being with their friends. They'll complain if they have to be with the 'little' kids." Many people are hesitant to try teaching combined-age groups because they're afraid kids will balk at something new. You can *let kids partner with same-age friends if they're really reluctant.* But at our field tests, we discovered that kids enjoyed being in combined-age Clue Crews. Sure, it was a little different at first, but as kids warmed up to their crew mates, we saw them working together, helping each other, and forming friendships. There were few complaints, and discipline problems were almost nonexistent.

A CLUE FOR YOU!

Churches around the country have reported great success with having families travel together as crews! Family crews build unity, encourage communication, and create wonderful memories that families will cherish for years to come.

A Clue for You!

You'll notice that all of the memory verses are from the book of John. Since children use the book of John as their Student Book, we selected passages that kids could look up, highlight, and tab during VBS. What a super way to make Bible memory meaningful, easy, and fun!

Day	Bible Point	Bible Story	Bible Verse
DAY 1	The Bible shows us the way to trust.	Peter walks to Jesus on the Sea of Galilee (Matthew 14:22-33).	"Do not let your hearts be troubled. Trust in God" (John 14:1a).
DAY 2	The Bible shows us the way to love.	Jesus washes the disciples' feet (John 13:1-17).	"A new command I give you: Love one another" (John 13:34a).
DAY 3	The Bible shows us the way to pray.	Jesus prays for his disciples and all believers, and then he is arrested (John 17:1–18:11).	"I pray also for those who will believe in me through their message, that all of them may be one" (John 17:20a-21b).
DAY 4	The Bible shows us the way to Jesus.	Jesus is crucified, rises again, and appears to Mary Magdalene (John 19:1–20:18).	"For God so loved the world that he gave his one and only Son, that whosoever believes in him shall not perish but have eternal life" (John 3:16).
DAY 5	The Bible shows us the way to live.	Paul stands firm in his faith, even in a shipwreck (Acts 27:1-44).	"If you love me, you will obey what I command" (John 14:15).

up and read the key verses during Chadder's Treasure Hunt Theater, it's a natural connection!

At each Discovery Site, kids will encounter a different presentation of the Bible Point, Bible story, or Bible verse.

Treasure Hunt Sing & Play

- The Treasure Hunt Sing & Play Leader repeats the Bible Point each day.
- In addition to fun praise songs, kids sing at least one song each day that specifically ties to that day's Bible Point. For example, on Day 4 children learn the song "Oh, How I Love Jesus" to go along with the Bible Point "The Bible shows us the way to Jesus."
- Each day kids learn a new verse of the Treasure Hunt Bible Adventure theme song, "I've Found Me a Treasure." Each day's verse focuses on the corresponding daily Bible story.
- Each day the Treasure Hunt Sing & Play Leader summarizes the daily Bible story.

A Clue for You!

You'll need to be available during Treasure Hunt Sing & Play. The Sing & Play Leader will send all the Clue Crew Leaders out of the room for a brief time of prayer with you. Then you'll come forward at the end of Sing & Play to give announcements, pray, and send Clue Crews to their first Discovery Sites.

Craft Cave

- The Craft Cave Leader repeats the Bible Point each day.
- Kids make crafts that remind them of each day's Bible story. For example, on Day 1 children make Jungle Gel to show them that amazing things happen when we trust.
- Kids listen to the Treasure Hunt Sing & Play songs as they're working.
- The Craft Cave Leader asks questions to help kids review and apply the Bible Point and the Bible story.
- Kids experience what it means to share the treasure of Jesus through Operation Kid-to-Kid.

Chadder's Treasure Hunt Theater

- In each day's video segment, Chadder Chipmunk hears the daily Bible Point and the Bible story.
- The Chadder's Treasure Hunt Theater Leader repeats the Bible Point each day.
- Kids apply Chadder's experiences to their own lives through role-play, problem-solving, and other short activities.
- Kids look up, read, and tab key Bible verses to see how the Bible guides us in life.

Treasure Treats

- The Treasure Treats Leader repeats the Bible Point each day.
- Kids make and eat snacks that reinforce the daily Bible story, such as Peter's Adventure Cakes (Day 1) and Sailboat Sandwiches (Day 5).
- Kids show God's love by serving others. Each day one set of Clue Crews makes the snacks for the entire VBS—even the preschoolers!
- Kids listen to Treasure Hunt Sing & Play songs as they make and eat their snacks.

Jungle Gym Games

- The Jungle Gym Games Leader repeats the Bible Point each day.
- Kids play games that encourage them to apply what they've learned. For example, on Day 1 kids apply the Bible Point, "The Bible shows us the way to love" by helping each other find and put on their shoes.
- Kids listen to Treasure Hunt Sing & Play songs as they play games.
- The Jungle Gym Games Leader connects each game to the daily Bible Point.

Bible Exploration

- The Bible Exploration Leader repeats the Bible Point each day.
- Kids experience the daily Bible story in a hands-on way. For example, on Day 2 kids experience what it's like to have their feet washed by their Clue Crew Leader.
- Kids discuss ways they can apply the daily Bible Point and Bible story to their lives. For example, on Day 3 they apply the Bible Point "The Bible shows us the way to pray" by praying in new and unique ways.

Treasure Time Finale

- The Treasure Time Finale Leader repeats the Bible Point each day.
- Kids repeat the Treasure Hunt Sing & Play songs they've learned that day.

A CLUE FOR YOU!

At each Discovery Site, kids will be carefully listening to hear the Bible Point so they can respond by shouting, "Eureka!" Watch their excitement and enthusiasm—and listening skills—build throughout the week!

● Kids use drama to apply what they've learned throughout the day. For example, on Day 4 children give their "sins" to "Jesus," who makes the sins disappear.

Preschool Bible Treasure Land

● Preschoolers sing the Treasure Hunt Sing & Play songs with the older kids.

● The Preschool Bible Treasure Land Leader tells each day's Bible story in a fun, involving way.

● The Preschool Bible Treasure Land Director repeats the Bible Point during each Treasure Land Discovery Site activity.

● Preschoolers hear the Bible story and the Bible Point as they watch *Chadder's Treasure Hunt Adventure.*

● Preschoolers make and eat snacks that reinforce the daily Bible story.

● Preschoolers sing additional songs that reinforce the daily Bible Point.

● Preschoolers participate in Treasure Time Finale with the older kids.

As you can see, Treasure Hunt Bible Adventure is packed with Bible-based activities your kids will love!

What's a DISCOVERY SITE?

At Treasure Hunt Bible Adventure, kids dig into Bible learning as they visit various Discovery Sites each day. Each Discovery Site features a different Bible-learning activity. Some Sites—such as Treasure Hunt Sing & Play, Treasure Treats, and Treasure Time Finale—accommodate all the Treasure Hunt Bible Adventure "explorers" simultaneously. Kids will visit other Discovery Sites in smaller groups.

Elementary-age kids visit the following Discovery Sites each day:

● Treasure Hunt Sing & Play
● Craft Cave
● Jungle Gym Games
● Treasure Treats
● Chadder's Treasure Hunt Theater
● Bible Exploration
● Treasure Time Finale

Preschoolers spend most of their time in the Preschool Bible Treasure Land, but they visit the following Discovery Sites each day:

● Treasure Hunt Sing & Play
● Chadder's Treasure Hunt Theater
● Treasure Time Finale

On Day 1 only, preschoolers skip Treasure Hunt Sing & Play and go straight to Preschool Bible Treasure Land. This allows little ones to meet their Preschool Director, Clue Crew Leaders, and Clue Crew members. Plus preschoolers get to make Treasure Treats on Day 1, and the extra time helps them accomplish this *big* task!

Each Discovery Site is staffed by an adult leader. If you have more than 150 kids in your program, you may want to assign two adult leaders to each Discovery Site. They can team teach a large group of kids or can set up identical Discovery Sites for two smaller groups in separate areas.

If you have up to 150 kids, your church might be set up like this…

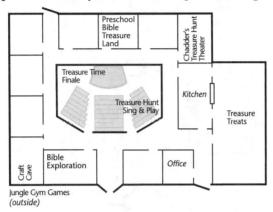

If you have more than 150 kids, your church might be set up like this…

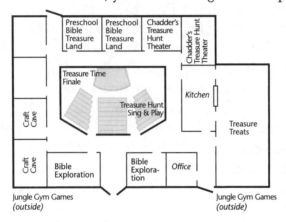

As you set up your Treasure Hunt Bible Adventure program, you assign kids to Clue Crews. On Day 1, kids report to their Clue Crews right away to start getting acquainted. Since Clue Crew members work closely during the week, Clue Crews encourage kids to make new friends at Treasure Hunt Bible Adventure. They also provide an organizational structure that helps kids progress from site to site in an orderly manner.

A CLUE FOR YOU!

For another large-group option, run a morning and evening program. Simply have participants sign up for the daytime or evening program; then decorate once and run two "shifts."

A CLUE FOR YOU!

Don't worry if you need to set up duplicate Discovery Sites—it's easy! If at all possible, place the duplicate stations next to each other. Then, when Clue Crews arrive at the stations, Discovery Site Leaders can simply direct half of them into each station.

A Clue for You!

Try to structure your Clue Crews so they contain no more than six members. Through field testing and customer feedback, we've discovered that larger crews can get unmanageable and become a frustration for the crew leader.

A Clue for You!

Important! Be sure to distribute the "For Clue Crew Leaders Only" handouts (pp. 113-116) to all crew leaders during your leader training time. Have extra handouts available at Treasure Hunt Bible Adventure for crew leaders who are unable to attend leader training. These handouts are a *valuable* source of helpful information to those who will work closely with children!

Clue Crews consist of three to five children and an adult or teenage Clue Crew Leader. If you're expecting visitors or want to encourage outreach, assign three children to each Clue Crew. Then encourage children to invite their friends to "fill up" their crews. If your attendance is pretty steady, assign up to five children to each crew. If possible, assign one child from each age level to each crew. "Your Clue Crew 'Family' " (p. 25), a developmental chart and illustrations, highlights the unique contribution children from each age level can make to a Clue Crew. The "Who's Who on the Crew?" chart on page 26 lists the five jobs Clue Crew members may fill during Treasure Hunt Bible Adventure.

Preschoolers' Clue Crews consist of up to five preschoolers and an adult or teenage crew leader.

Detailed instructions for setting up Clue Crews begin on page 137. Qualifications for crew leaders are listed on page 94.

YOUR CLUE CREW "FAMILY"

I just finished kindergarten. I'm a unique and important part of my Clue Crew because I have a great imagination. I can help my Clue Crew pretend we're really on a rain forest expedition.

I just finished first grade. I'm a unique and important part of my Clue Crew because I like to be the best. I can help encourage my Clue Crew to be the best it can be.

I just finished third grade. I'm a unique and important part of my Clue Crew because I like to be challenged. I can help younger members of my Clue Crew with challenging projects.

I just finished second grade. I'm a unique and important part of my Clue Crew because I want everything to be fair. I can help make sure we all take turns and treat each other fairly.

I just finished fourth grade. I'm a unique and important part of my Clue Crew because I like to ask questions. I can help my Clue Crew ask questions to make sure we understand what we're learning.

I just finished fifth grade. I'm a unique and important part of my Clue Crew because I like to make choices. I can help my Clue Crew make choices about a crew name, jobs, and activities.

TREASURE HUNT BIBLE ADVENTURE BASICS

Permission to photocopy this chart from Group's Treasure Hunt Bible Adventure: Treasure Hunt Bible Adventure Director Manual granted for local church use. Copyright © Group Publishing, Inc., P.O. Box 481, Loveland, CO 80539.

Who's Who on THE CREW?

A Clue for You!

Each Clue Crew will need one Clue Crew treasure bag in which to carry its Student Books and crafts. Clue Crew treasure bags are available from Group Publishing and your local Christian bookstore.

During Treasure Hunt Sing & Play on Day 1, kids choose Clue Crew jobs and place job stickers (from the Treasure Hunt sticker sheets) on their name badges. You can expect each of the following jobs to be represented in each Clue Crew. If crews have fewer than five kids, some kids may have more than one job.

In addition to the five jobs listed below, each crew should have an adult or teenage crew leader. You can count on the crew leader to help kids complete the activities at each Discovery Site.

Kids are excited about having special jobs! Each leader manual suggests ways Discovery Site Leaders can call on kids to fulfill the job responsibilities they've chosen.

A Clue for You!

As VBS Director, you'll find that open, clear communication is your best friend! Be sure to touch base with the Sing & Play Leader to remind him or her to allow time for children to choose their roles on Day 1. Although this process is written into the Treasure Hunt Sing & Play Leader Manual, it's good to double-check and be sure the leader understands the importance of this process.

Jobs	Duties
READER	• likes to read • reads Bible passages aloud
CLUE KEEPER	• collects the Treasure Chest Quest Clues • chooses action ideas for traveling between Discovery Sites (such as shuffling, skipping, hopping, galloping, or marching) • helps monitor the daily schedule to let the Clue Crew know what's coming next
MATERIALS MANAGER	• likes to pass out and collect supplies • passes out and collects Student Books • carries the crew's treasure bag until the day is over
CHEERLEADER	• likes to smile and make people happy • makes sure people use kind words and actions • leads group in cheering during Jungle Gym Games
PRAYER PERSON	• likes to pray and isn't afraid to pray aloud • makes sure the group takes time to pray each day • leads or opens prayer times

Where Do Middle SCHOOLERS FIT IN?

Many churches are unsure how to handle upper-elementary kids; they seem too old for some children's ministry programs and too young for youth group. With Treasure Hunt Bible Adventure, upper-elementary kids can fill a number of roles. Check out the following options to find the perfect fit for your middle schoolers. They can

● **join Clue Crews as Assistant Clue Crew Leaders.** Many upper-elementary kids are ready for simple leadership roles, but they still enjoy participating in activities such as games, snack time, crafts, and biblical dramas. As Assistant Clue Crew Leaders, they can help their crew leaders by keeping kids together, working with younger children during Craft Cave, or doing the more difficult jobs during Treasure Treats service.

● **become Assistant Discovery Site Leaders.** Your middle schoolers are developing their gifts and talents and are discovering the things they excel at and enjoy. Being an Assistant Discovery Site Leader is a great way to encourage kids toward this discovery. Do you know an older child who's developing a love for drama and storytelling? Use him or her as an Assistant Treasure Time Finale Leader or an Assistant Bible Exploration Leader. What about a child who enjoys sports and other athletic activities? Ask him or her to be an Assistant Jungle Gym Games Leader. Your Discovery Site Leaders will love the extra help, and older kids will enjoy the added responsibility.

● **help with Preschool Bible Treasure Land registration.** Some middle schoolers are nurturing and caring—great qualities for helping preschoolers find their way at Treasure Hunt Bible Adventure. For the first day or two, have a few upper-elementary kids available to help preschoolers find their Clue Crew Leaders, show preschoolers the restroom, or play with a shy child to get him or her accustomed to Preschool Bible Treasure Land.

● **create an upper-elementary Sing-Along Crew.** Older children (who might normally hesitate to sing and move to music) will enjoy teaching song motions and leading younger children in Treasure Hunt Sing & Play. Ask a group of upper-elementary kids to work with the Treasure Hunt Sing & Play Leader to learn the words and motions to all thirteen Treasure Hunt Bible Adventure songs. The Sing-Along Crew will add visual excitement and energy to your singing time.

Middle schoolers have so much to offer (and gain from) your program! We've heard countless stories of middle schoolers and teenagers whose lives were changed because of their experience in leading or assisting in VBS. The more these kids are involved in your program, the more opportunities you have to touch their lives.

Field Test Findings

It's important that upper-elementary kids understand the specifics of their jobs. We discovered that assigning kids this age as "Floaters" who could fill in wherever there was a need gave them too much freedom and not enough direction. Our upper-elementary Floaters wandered around and complained about being bored. When we gave them specific roles, such as Assistant Chef or Assistant Craft Cave Leader, they did a super job of helping out!

Field Test Findings

Make sure you choose more mature fifth- and sixth-graders for leadership roles. Many kids this age still enjoy being crew members and participating in all activities. In our field test, we assumed that one fifth-grade boy would make a great preschool crew leader. As it turned out, he felt slighted because he couldn't make his own cool craft or participate fully in other activities. Be sure to ask kids what they'd like to do instead of assuming they'd rather opt "out."

Field Test Findings

Who says VBS is just for little kids? We've heard so many stories of how teenagers' lives were touched by past VBS programs. Young adults who volunteered had such a great time and were so moved by the Bible experiences, they made life-changing decisions!

Field Test Findings

We've discovered that younger children really look up to teenagers and young adults. In fact, you may find that crew members and teenage Clue Crew Leaders form close friendships and work well together. We frequently saw high-school-age crew leaders letting crew members wear their crew leader caps. Crew members thought they were hot stuff!

Do Teenagers Have a Role at TREASURE HUNT BIBLE ADVENTURE?

Teenagers have an important role in making Treasure Hunt Bible Adventure a successful expedition! Use the following suggestions to involve teenagers (or college students) in your program:

• **Have them act as Clue Crew Leaders.** Many young adults have younger siblings or baby-sit frequently and are comfortable working with children. Young adults will have a great time leading their crews—and will love how easy it is. (Teenagers will actually get as much out of the Bible stories and discussions as the young children will!)

• **Let teenagers and young adults help with registration.** Believe it or not, some young people have excellent organizational skills. These young people enjoy forming crews, greeting children, and helping kids find their Clue Crew Leaders. After the first day, your registration helpers can register newcomers, count the daily attendance and report the number to the Treasure Treats Leader, and fill in for crew leaders who are absent.

• **Have qualified teenagers run your sound system or act as photographers.** Some high school drama programs train young people how to run sound, lighting, and video equipment. These teenagers make excellent Treasure Hunt Bible Adventure technical staff members. You may even ask them to put together a slide show or video production of your program!

• **Ask teenagers to act as Bible Exploration volunteers.** The Bible Exploration Leader needs several volunteers to act as Bible characters in simple dramas. Teenagers with dramatic flair enjoy playing Mary, Habib, or prison guards.

• **If your church's youth group has a choir or worship band, let it help with Treasure Hunt Sing & Play and Treasure Time Finale.** Kids at Treasure Hunt Bible Adventure love singing with the "big kids," and young adults will never have such a receptive and friendly audience again! Your Discovery Site Leaders enjoy the extra backup and enthusiasm. Plus teenagers learn and grow right along with the children!

There are countless ways to involve youth in Treasure Hunt Bible Adventure. Just let teenagers fill in where their gifts, talents, or interests lead them! You'll be surprised at how committed and enthusiastic these young volunteers are.

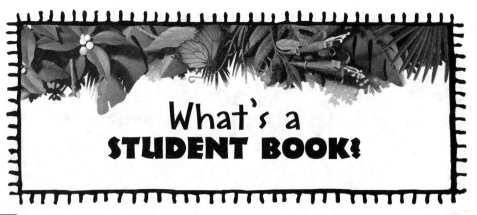

What's a STUDENT BOOK?

Each child at Treasure Hunt Bible Adventure will need a Student Book. The elementary Student Book is the Gospel of John, taken from The New Adventure Bible. This easy-to-understand Bible translation is filled with age-appropriate study helps, interesting Bible facts, and short devotional thoughts. Kids will dig in to practical Bible study skills—learning how to read, highlight, and create helpful tabs for finding important verses long after VBS.

Each Student Book also contains a Spanish translation of the Gospel of John. Kids will mark key passages in this Bible, and create a cool Operation Kid-to-Kid Magnetic Bookmark to go inside it. Then, at the end of the week, children will remove their Spanish Bible books from their Student Books and present them as an offering at Treasure Time Finale. You can give the books to a Spanish-speaking church in your area, send on a missions trip to South America, or send the books to International Bible Society for world-wide distribution. For more options, check out page 38 of this manual. This is a meaningful, hands-on way for kids to share God's Word with others.

Field Test Findings

It was neat to see how much kids truly treasured their Bible books! Weeks after our field test, a local pastor (of a different church) shared how his eight-year-old daughter had brought home her Bible book and excitedly explained how he could find important verses to help him trust, love, pray, know Jesus, and live.

Preschoolers have their own age-appropriate Student Books, each complete with five illustrated Bible stories and activity pages to make Bible learning fun and memorable. Preschoolers' parents will appreciate the take-home newsletters—full of easy follow-up ideas, fun Bible-learning songs, and simple crafts that reinforce each day's Bible story and Point.

A CLUE FOR YOU!

You'll want to provide a Treasure Hunt sticker sheet for each child (elementary and preschool) at your VBS. These sticker sheets include all the stickers kids will need for crafts and for their Student Books. Kids will love the bright, fun designs, and you'll love finding everything in one place!

Preschoolers will look forward to adding stickers to their Bible books, just like the "big kids." They'll even add stickers to the Spanish-translations of the Gospel of John, to help Spanish-speaking children find key passages in their Bibles.

Who Is CHADDER CHIPMUNK™?

Chadder Chipmunk is a lovable, mischievous character the kids love. Each day when kids visit Chadder's Treasure Hunt Theater, they view a segment of *Chadder's Treasure Hunt Adventure*.

Kids enjoy exploring with Chadder as he seeks treasures of gold and riches, only to discover that Jesus is the greatest treasure of all. Though children of all ages laugh at Chadder's antics as he stumbles from clue to clue, they also discover important Bible truths that apply to everyday life.

Chadder Chipmunk explains that he's excited to go treasure hunting with his friends, Hayley and Tim. Unfortunately, two bumbling thieves, Ned and Pete, hear about the treasure and follow the kids, intending to steal the treasure after the kids and Chadder find it. As they follow the map, the treasure hunters discover a ship, the SS Hope, that's being prepared for a journey to help children along the river. First Mate Ryan helps Chadder and the kids, while Wally the parrot warns them of Riverboat Bob. As the adventure continues, Ryan guides the kids and Chadder, teaching them that the Bible is a treasure map which shows us the way to the treasure of Jesus. In the end, Chadder, Tim, and Hayley befriend Riverboat Bob and decide to give their treasure to Colonel Mike and the mission of the SS Hope.

The Chadder's Treasure Hunt Theater Leader Manual contains discussion questions and activities that go along with each day's segment of *Chadder's Treasure Hunt Adventure*. The video is available from Group Publishing and your local Christian bookstore.

A CLUE FOR YOU!

Your kids will love Chadder and will look forward to seeing him! Not only will they enjoy the twists and turns of the story, but they'll appreciate the wonderful downtime during a busy day at Treasure Hunt Bible Adventure. Kids are so active during VBS that it's nice for them to have a few moments to sit down, cool off, and relax. (Your Clue Crew Leaders will appreciate it, too!)

Can Kids Really Make THEIR OWN SNACKS?

Each day at Treasure Hunt Bible Adventure, a different group of kids prepares snacks for the entire VBS. Snack preparation provides kids a unique opportunity to live out the daily Bible Point by serving others. And it makes your job easier because you don't have to recruit additional volunteers to make snacks.

Believe it or not, one-fourth of your kids *can* prepare snacks for everyone else—if you follow the field-tested, step-by-step instructions provided in the Treasure Treats Leader Manual. Each day, snack preparation will follow the simple procedures outlined below.

1. Before kids arrive, the Treasure Treats Leader sets out supplies according to the diagrams provided in the Treasure Treats Leader Manual.

2. After kids arrive and wash their hands, the leader explains each step of the snack preparation and invites kids to choose which steps they'd like to work on.

3. Kids work in assembly lines to prepare the snacks. Clue Crew Leaders are assigned the more difficult tasks such as handling sharp knives or pouring drinks.

4. Kids set out the completed snacks on tables, where they'll be picked up and gobbled down during Treasure Treats.

Kids who serve on the Treasure Treats Service Crew report for snack preparation right after Treasure Hunt Sing & Play. They'll take twenty to twenty-five minutes to prepare snacks before moving on to their next Discovery Site. And just in case kids don't finish in time, the Treasure Treats Leader has an additional twenty to twenty-five minutes to make final preparations before all the children arrive to eat. In Treasure Hunt Bible Adventure field tests, even preschoolers were able to complete their snack preparation within the allotted time!

As Treasure Hunt Director, you'll want to drop in on the Treasure Treats Service Crew each day. Ask the leader how kids' work is progressing, and affirm the children for a job well done. But don't linger too long; you may distract kids from completing their work. Be sure to return at snack time to see children explain the meaning of the snack as *they* teach the Bible Point. Then watch the Treasure Treats Service Crew kids' faces light up as they're recognized for their accomplishment!

Field Test Findings

In our field test, Treasure Treats Service became something kids really looked forward to. At the end of each day's Treasure Hunt Sing & Play, the Treasure Hunt Bible Adventure Director would announce which group would be preparing the snack that day. You could hear the "lucky" kids whisper, "Yeah!" "All right!" or "That's us!" within their crews. We think it was terrific that kids looked forward to serving others.

What Is OPERATION KID-TO-KID™?

More Than an Offering

In developing Treasure Hunt Bible Adventure, the VBS team at Group Publishing wanted to include a meaningful service project that would help kids realize that with God's help, even children can impact the world! From customer feedback, we learned that VBS Directors (like you) wanted kids to give more than money. They wanted kids to give something that was meaningful and tangible—something that would meet the needs of children across the world.

We met with International Bible Society, an organization with a heart for reaching people with God's Word. It's partnership with other Bible translators have resulted in the publication of 166 New Testaments and 1,283 Scripture publications in 506 languages. IBS places Bibles in the hands of millions, from every corner of the world! When we approached the staff and talked about working together, IBS caught the vision and joined Operation Kid-to-Kid.

How Your Kids Can Help

First of all, determine where you'll focus your mission. Last year, some VBS Directors let us know that they wanted a missions project that would affect children right in their own communities. Others preferred a more international project. Operation Kid-to-Kid is easy to adapt for any situation. So choose where you'll send the Spanish translations of the Gospel of John; then get kids excited about the need they'll meet.

Each child will find a Spanish translation of the Gospel of John in his or her Student Book. During the week, kids will highlight and mark key passages in their own Bible books as well as in the Spanish Bible books. In Craft Cave, kids will each create a fun Operation Kid-to-Kid Magnetic Bible Bookmark. Aside from being useful and fun, the bookmark shows how the Bible draws us together even when distance or language barriers keep us apart. Kids place the bookmark at Juan 3:16; then they present the Spanish Bible books as an offering during the last Treasure Time Finale.

This is a powerful, moving ceremony. Kids and leaders will be amazed as they watch the "mountain" of Bible books grow higher and higher. It's a very concrete

DID YOU KNOW?
Of the estimated 6,500 languages spoken today, more than 4,000 of them represent 350 million people who have no Scripture in their mother tongue.

Field Test Findings

We discovered that kids need a small-group setting to discuss, understand, and focus on Operation Kid-to-Kid. Craft Cave is a natural "Operation Kid-to-Kid Headquarters." There, children learn about the project and its impact, and create the Operation Kid-to-Kid Bible Bookmarks. In Craft Cave, kids also "meet" three children (through "Operation Kid-to-Kid" posters) who are representatives of the children who will receive the Bibles.

way for kids to see that it's easy to share the treasure of Jesus.

After Treasure Hunt Bible Adventure, it's time to distribute the Bibles! You can do one of the following:

● Have families deliver them, door-to-door, to Spanish-speaking families in or near your community.

● Have children take them to a bilingual, Spanish-speaking church in or near your community. Allow the kids to play Jungle Gym games, lead Sing & Play songs, watch the *Chadder's Treasure Hunt Bible Adventure* video, and enjoy Treasure Treats together.

● Send the books along with your youth (or another group) on a missions trip. Many groups take missions trips to Mexico or South America, where people speak Spanish. This is a super way for your kids to support a missions team in a tangible way.

● Send the books to International Bible Society for worldwide distribution. Simply place the packs in a large, sturdy box and tape it shut. Affix the mailing label from the Operation Kid-to-Kid brochure (in the Treasure Hunt Bible Adventure Starter Kit), and ship the box to Operation Kid-to-Kid, c/o International Bible Society, 1820 Jet Stream Drive, Colorado Springs, CO 80921. They'll take care of the rest!

Planning for OPERATION KID-TO-KID™

Before TREASURE HUNT BIBLE ADVENTURE

● **Determine who will receive the Spanish Bible books.** Check with local agencies, missions organizations, your church board, or community leaders to find out about groups that may be able to give the Bible books to Spanish-speaking children.

● **Publicize your program.** Let your congregation know that the kids in your church will be sharing God's Word with children in your community or around the world! Use the "Operation Kid-to-Kid" posters to help people understand that children in twenty four countries may be affected by your program! You may want to have a special offering to help fund your Student Book purchases.

● **Let the community know.** Photocopy the "Operation Kid-to-Kid™ News Release" on page 39, and fill in the information regarding your church's program. Send the news release to local newspapers, television, and radio stations so they can let others in your community know about your participation in Operation Kid-to-Kid.

During TREASURE HUNT BIBLE ADVENTURE

● **Remind kids of the importance of their mission.** Often, kids in North America take their Bibles for granted. Many children have more than one Bible and rarely explore the riches inside. Help children understand that the Bible is a map that leads us to the most valuable treasure ever—Jesus! Let them know that they can share that treasure with children around the world!

● **Check in with Clue Crew Leaders.** During your opening huddle and prayer with the Clue Crew Leaders, ask them how kids are responding to Operation Kid-to-Kid. You may suggest that Clue Crew Leaders teach their crew members a few simple words of Spanish, or talk about how important it is for everyone to read God's Word.

● **Encourage kids to pray for their "Bible partners."** During Treasure Hunt Sing & Play, or in Treasure Time Finale, allow a short time for kids to pray

A CLUE FOR YOU!

You may want to provide another set of "Operation Kid-to-Kid" posters for your Preschool Bible Treasure Land. Preschoolers will enjoy meeting the children on the posters, too. These posters are available from Group Publishing and your local Christian bookstore.

Field Test Findings

In our field test, we were amazed and delighted to see that kids really did get excited by their Student Bible books. This excitement and pride brought about a natural desire to share the good news with others. As a result, kids took Operation Kid-to-Kid very seriously, realizing that this was an opportunity to share their enthusiasm with others.

for the children who will receive the Spanish Bible books. Children can pray that the Bible recipients (or their "Bible partners") will learn that Jesus is the greatest treasure ever!

After TREASURE HUNT BIBLE ADVENTURE

● **Send your Spanish Bible books to the Kid-to-Kid Send-Off Center.** Place your Spanish Bible books with bookmarks in a large, sturdy packing box. Stuff the box with newspaper or newsprint to keep the books from shifting or possibly tearing. Tape the box shut, and affix the mailing label from the Operation Kid-to-Kid brochure in your Starter Kit. (Offering envelopes are available if your church wishes to take a donation to cover your shipping expenses, IBS's shipping expenses, or as a gift to the organization.)

● **Look for your Operation Kid-to-Kid update.** If you choose to send your Bible books to IBS, IBS will send your church a newsletter about Operation Kid-to-Kid several months after your program. You'll learn how this outreach program affected thousands of children around the world. Share this powerful information with your children; they'll love hearing that their "treasure maps" went around the world to share the treasure of Jesus!

● **Remind kids to visit the Operation Kid-to-Kid Web site.** Technology today will allow kids to chat with other Operation Kid-to-Kid participants and learn more about the countries where the school kits may be sent. Children will enjoy visiting the Operation Kid-to-Kid Web site (www.OK2K.org).

Operation Kid-to-Kid™ News Release

Adapt the information in this news release to fit your church's Treasure Hunt Bible Adventure program. Then submit typed, double-spaced copies to your local newspapers, radio stations, and TV stations. You may want to check with them for any other specific requirements regarding news releases.

[Name of church] will be involved in a worldwide mission project called Operation Kid-to-Kid™. For this project, children attending [name of church]'s Treasure Hunt Bible Adventure will send Spanish translations of the Gospel of John to Spanish-speaking children around the world.

Operation Kid-to-Kid will show kids that, even though we're separated by language and distance, everyone can share the treasure of Jesus! Kids in North America will add special stickers and tabs to key Bible verses, plus create a magnetic bookmark to place inside the Spanish Bible book. The Bibles will be shipped to International Bible Society, which will distribute them to children in Spanish-speaking countries around the world.

Operation Kid-to-Kid is just one part of Treasure Hunt Bible Adventure, a program in which kids learn that the Bible is like a treasure map, leading us to Jesus—the greatest treasure of all. Treasure Hunt Bible Adventure begins [starting date] and continues through [ending date]. It's located at [name of church and church address]. Registration opens each day at [starting time] and closes at [ending time]. For more information, call [church phone number].

MAPPING OUT YOUR TREASURE HUNT BIBLE ADVENTURE

How to Create a RADICAL RAIN FOREST

Planning CALENDAR

Three to Six Months Before TREASURE HUNT BIBLE ADVENTURE

○ **Begin praying for your church's Treasure Hunt Bible Adventure.** Ask God to prepare the hearts of church members, workers, and children who will attend.

○ **Choose a format for your Treasure Hunt Bible Adventure.**
✔ Will you meet in the morning or in the evening?
✔ Will you meet every day for a week or once a week for several weeks?
✔ Will your program be for children only or will entire families be invited to attend?
✔ Will you meet at your church or another location?

○ **Set Treasure Hunt Bible Adventure dates.** As you're considering dates, you may want to find out about other summer programs offered by your church or your community so you can avoid conflicts.

○ **Choose a Treasure Hunt Director.** If you're reading this manual, that's you! The director is responsible for planning, recruiting staff, and overseeing all details to ensure that Treasure Hunt Bible Adventure goes smoothly.

○ **Set a budget.** Your church may already include VBS in its budget. If so, find out what funds are available. If your church doesn't have a VBS budget in place, consider the following ideas:
✔ Collect an offering to cover expenses.
✔ Charge a per-child registration fee for Treasure Hunt Bible Adventure. Give discounts to families that register more than one child.
✔ Invite congregation members to "sponsor" children by contributing a per-child amount. (See the "Registration" section on pages 133-150 for more specifics on this idea.)
✔ Hold a creative fund-raiser! Open your own "Rain Forest Cafe" (your basic bake sale) or hold a monthlong treasure hunt (penny collection). Not only will this raise funds for your program, but it will get everyone excited about your Treasure Hunt Bible Adventure!

A CLUE FOR YOU!
We frequently hear back from customers who hold a very "nontraditional" VBS—using different settings, times, or dates. Be creative and choose the best VBS setting for your church situation!

Two to Three Months Before
TREASURE HUNT BIBLE ADVENTURE

○ **Plan Treasure Hunt Bible Adventure publicity.** Decide how you'll promote Treasure Hunt Bible Adventure in your church and community. Refer to the "Publicity: Getting Your Church and Community 'Clued In' " section (pp. 119-131) in this manual for publicity ideas and resources.

○ **Begin recruiting Discovery Site Leaders.** Photocopy the leader job descriptions (pp. 85-92). Give the job descriptions to people in your church who'd enjoy leading a Discovery Site. Or post the job descriptions on a large bulletin board you've covered with jungle wrapping paper or a huge treasure map. As you talk to people, focus on the job descriptions rather than on previous church teaching experience. A restaurant chef who's never taught Sunday school might make a great Treasure Treats Leader! We've heard from lots of VBS Directors who say that this program is a great way to involve people who don't think they have anything to offer children! (And once they've tried it, they're hooked!)

You might want to announce your staffing needs in a worship service. Then post the job descriptions on a large sheet of poster board under the heading "Wanted: People To Help Kids Discover Jesus." People can sign their names on the job descriptions they're interested in. It's OK if more than one person signs up for each Discovery Site. Team teaching is the way to go!

○ **Estimate your Treasure Hunt Bible Adventure enrollment.** Use figures from your church's Sunday school or figures from last year's VBS program. Once you've estimated how many children will attend, figure out how many Clue Crew Leaders you'll need. You'll need one adult or teenage Clue Crew Leader for every five children, including preschoolers. Be sure to have extra Clue Crew Leaders ready in case you need to form Clue Crews from last-minute registrants.

○ **Order Treasure Hunt Bible Adventure materials.** If you purchased the Treasure Hunt Bible Adventure Starter Kit, you already have a leader manual for every Discovery Site. You may want to order additional leader manuals for team teaching. Your Chadder's Treasure Hunt Theater Leader will need a copy of the *Chadder's Treasure Hunt Adventure* video.

For every elementary-age child, you'll *need* to order
- ✔ an Elementary Student Book;
- ✔ an elementary Treasure Hunt sticker sheet; and
- ✔ craft items:
  - ✔ a Jungle Gel Cell,
  - ✔ two yards of Mini Jungle Vines,
- ✔ an Operation Kid-to-Kid Magnetic Bookmark,
- ✔ one Good News Treasure Pouch,
- ✔ four Good News beads (yellow, red, green, white),
- ✔ one Surprise Treasure Chest Kit, and
- ✔ one Rain Forest Creature.

Field Test Findings

We've heard it from customers, and it's even happening to us! Our first VBS field test averaged about seventy-five kids per day. During the second program, we grew to a little over one hundred per day. When we tested our next program, we averaged about 150 per day. This year we were unprepared for the 170 children who arrived on the first day! All we can say is that we'll prepare for the masses *next year!*

MAPPING OUT YOUR ADVENTURE

For every preschooler, you'll *need* to order
- a Preschool Student Book;
- a preschool Treasure Hunt sticker sheet; and
- craft items:
  - one Jungle Gel Cell,
  - two yards of Mini Jungle Vines,
  - an Operation Kid-to-Kid Magnetic Bookmark,
  - one Good News Treasure Pouch, and
  - one Surprise Treasure Chest Kit.

Even if you're planning a late-summer program, it's not too early to order materials! As you update your registration count, you can order additional student supplies as needed.

○ Survey your church facilities. Make preliminary Discovery Site area assignments. You'll need to set up a separate room or area for each site. Use the following guidelines:

○ **Treasure Hunt Sing & Play**
- large room to accommodate all the adventurers (possibly a sanctuary or fellowship hall)
- sound system/microphone (helpful)
- outlet to plug in audiocassette player or CD player (or a sound system to play *Treasure Hunt Sing & Play* audiocassette or CD)
- outlet to plug in overhead projector (if using *Treasure Hunt Sing & Play Transparencies*)

○ **Chadder's Treasure Hunt Theater**
- classroom to accommodate all the preschoolers at once and to accommodate one-fourth of the elementary-age kids (helpful if room can be darkened)
- outlet to plug in TV/VCR

○ **Craft Cave**
- classroom to accommodate one-fourth of the elementary-age kids
- one or two low tables (helpful)
- outlet to plug in audiocassette player or CD player if using *Treasure Hunt Sing & Play* audiocassette or CD

○ **Treasure Treats**
- large room to accommodate entire Treasure Hunt Bible Adventure (possibly a fellowship hall or gymnasium)
- church kitchen or other noncarpeted area for Treasure Treats Service

○ **Jungle Gym Games**
- room or outdoor area to accommodate one-fourth of the elementary-age kids (a fellowship hall, gymnasium, lawn, or parking lot)
- room enough for children to run around
- outlet to plug in audiocassette player or CD player if using *Treasure Hunt Sing & Play* audiocassette or CD

A Clue For You!

If your plans involve more than 150 children, consider running two or more simultaneous Discovery Sites. For more information on how to do this, see "What's a Discovery Site?" (p. 22).

Field Test Findings

We had children pick up their snacks inside after praying together and learning the meaning of the snack. Then children went directly outside to eat. This was less messy, gave children the opportunity to enjoy the sunshine, and provided a few crumbs for the birds!

○ **Bible Exploration**
  ✔ classroom that can accommodate one-fourth of the elementary-age kids and that can be darkened
  ✔ classroom that's larger than 10x25 feet
  ✔ classroom that's in a quiet area of your facility (helpful for storytelling, especially on Day 4)
  ✔ outlet to plug in audiocassette player

○ **Treasure Time Finale**
  ✔ large room to accommodate entire Treasure Hunt Bible Adventure (possibly a sanctuary or fellowship hall; could use the same room as Treasure Hunt Sing & Play)
  ✔ sound system/microphone (helpful)
  ✔ outlet to plug in audiocassette player
  ✔ stage (helpful)

○ **Preschool Bible Treasure Land**
  ✔ classroom(s) to accommodate all preschoolers
  ✔ outlet to plug in audiocassette player
  ✔ restroom facilities in room or nearby
  ✔ child-sized furniture
  ✔ preschool toys such as blocks, modeling dough, dress-up clothes, and stuffed animals

A Clue for You!
Since preschoolers work at learning centers or sites, you may want to set up one room for these sites and use another place for storytelling and singing.

A Clue for You!
If you can't arrange for all your leaders to make it to your leader training meeting, consider videotaping the meeting. Send copies of the videotape to volunteers who couldn't make it. If you can't videotape the session, send the *Discover!* video to your leaders to better prepare them for their roles.

○ **Plan and schedule a leader training meeting using the " 'Gearing Up for Adventure!' Leader Training Meeting" (p. 104).** This outline incorporates the *Discover!* video, which contains clips from our Treasure Hunt Bible Adventure field test. Your Discovery Site Leaders will enjoy seeing Treasure Hunt Bible Adventure in action. Be sure to include Clue Crew Leaders in your training so they can better understand their role. The *Discover!* video includes a section just for crew leaders that explains their duties and describes how to be effective in discussions and with discipline.

Plan to meet for at least two hours.

Eight Weeks Before TREASURE HUNT BIBLE ADVENTURE

○ **Begin recruiting Clue Crew Leaders.** Clue Crew Leaders are like older brothers and sisters in the Clue Crew family. They aren't responsible for teaching, and they don't have to prepare anything. Clue Crew Leaders can be teenagers, college students, parents, or grandparents. They need only to love the Lord and love children.

Clue Crew Leaders should plan to participate in Treasure Hunt Bible Adventure for the entire program. If they need to be absent one or more days, encourage them to find their own substitutes.

○ **Begin publicity.** Fill in your program's dates and times on the Treasure Hunt Bible Adventure outdoor banner (available from Group Publishing and your local Christian bookstore). Display the banner in a prominent outdoor location.

Hang Treasure Hunt Bible Adventure theme posters (available from Group Publishing and your local Christian bookstore) in your church and community.

Show the promotional segment of the *Discover!* video during a worship service or other church gathering. This five-minute segment, found at the beginning of your *Discover!* video, shows scenes from an actual Treasure Hunt Bible Adventure program. You'll find that the video helps build enthusiasm, recruit volunteers, and promote attendance for your program.

○ **Begin gathering supplies.** Refer to the master supply list, "Supplies: Everything You Need for an Exciting Expedition" (p. 59). Consult with Discovery Site Leaders to inform them of how you'll handle supply collection. Will you gather all supplies or will each leader gather his or her own supplies? You may want to ask church members to donate food supplies (such as cupcakes, pretzel rods, or gummy bears) or easy-to-find items (such as inner tubes or robes).

○ **Plan your Treasure Hunt Bible Adventure schedule.** The average VBS program runs for up to three hours each day. Group's Treasure Hunt Bible Adventure materials have been developed with these parameters in mind. For a three-hour program, Treasure Hunt Sing & Play and Treasure Treats should last fifteen minutes apiece, and every other Discovery Site should last twenty-five minutes. See the daily schedules on pages 74-80 to see how this works. If your program will meet for more or less time than three hours each day, you'll need to adapt these times accordingly.

Four Weeks Before TREASURE HUNT BIBLE ADVENTURE

○ **Recruit additional volunteers.** In addition to Discovery Site Leaders and Clue Crew Leaders, you may want to recruit volunteers to help with registration, transportation, photography, and child care for the staff.

○ **Continue publicity.** Mail Treasure Hunt Bible Adventure invitation postcards to children in your church and community. Distribute Treasure Hunt Bible Adventure doorknob danglers in your community. Write your church's name and when your Treasure Hunt Bible Adventure will begin.

○ **Begin preregistration.** Photocopy the "Treasure Hunt Bible Adventure Registration Form" (p. 150), or purchase Treasure Hunt Bible Adventure registration cards (available from Group Publishing and your local Christian bookstore). Insert copies in your church bulletins, distribute copies in Sunday school classes, and keep a supply in your church office. Encourage parents from your church to preregister their children and their children's friends. This will make your first day more manageable.

A Clue for You!

It's a good idea to line up a few extra Clue Crew Leaders who will be available in case you have lots of walk-in registrants. Be sure these Clue Crew Leaders arrive early on Day 1 so they can step in if necessary. (Because no preparation is needed for Clue Crew Leaders, it's easy for people to step in at any point.)

Field Test Findings

Our Discovery Site Leaders needed a way to quickly identify the Clue Crew Leaders in each group. We provided Treasure Hunt Bible Adventure caps for the crew leaders to wear during the week. Many crew leaders wrote their names on their caps, used markers to decorate their caps, or had their Clue Crew members sign their caps. The caps became fun souvenirs for crew leaders to take home at the end of the week. Treasure Hunt Bible Adventure caps are available from Group Publishing and your local Christian bookstore.

○ **Hold the scheduled leader training meeting.** Plan to meet in a large room where you'll be able to try out some Treasure Hunt Bible Adventure snacks and activities. Before the meeting, set up a TV and VCR, and decorate the room using the suggestions provided in the leader training outline (p. 105). Bring the Discovery Site leader manuals and photocopies of the "For Clue Crew Leaders Only" handouts (pp. 113-118). Don't forget to provide yummy Treasure Treats for your workers!

○ **Meet with each Discovery Site Leader.** It's a good idea to touch base with each Discovery Site Leader on a one-to-one basis. Take each person to lunch, out for ice cream, or simply go for a walk together as you discuss what supplies the leaders need, what concerns they may have, or any aspects of the program they're not clear on. Not only will this prevent miscommunication, but it will help your volunteers know how much you appreciate them!

○ **Provide Treasure Hunt Bible Adventure information to your church office.** Fill in your church's information on the community flier on page 129, and photocopy a stack of completed fliers on brightly colored paper to put in your church office. Someone in the office can refer to the fliers if people call with questions about your program and can distribute fliers to people who stop by the office.

If your church has a phone answering machine, you may also want to include Treasure Hunt Bible Adventure information in your recorded message. If your church has its own Web site, be sure to add Treasure Hunt Bible Adventure information there, too.

Two Weeks Before TREASURE HUNT BIBLE ADVENTURE

○ **Check your registration count.** Make sure you have enough Student Books and Treasure Hunt sticker sheets for each child to have one. Order extras just in case; many churches experience last-minute add-ons, first-day surprises, and unexpected increases as kids bring their friends throughout the week. Also double-check that you have enough Clue Crew Leaders, assigning one crew leader to five children.

○ **Check your supply collection.** Make a final announcement or put a final supply list in your church bulletin. Gather or purchase additional supplies as necessary.

○ **Continue publicity.** Photocopy and fill out the news release (p. 128), and send copies to your local newspapers, radio sites, and TV sites. Use the snazzy clip art found on the *Treasure Hunt Sing & Play Music & Clip Art CD* to create fliers, bulletins, posters, and more! This CD contains the thirteen upbeat Treasure Hunt Sing & Play songs and works with Macintosh and PC-compatible computers.

Announce Treasure Hunt Bible Adventure in worship services and other

church gatherings. Put bulletin inserts and table tents (pp. 125-126) in your church's worship bulletins.

As church members enter your facility, distribute theme-oriented snacks such as foil-covered chocolate coins, Hershey's Nuggets candies, candy necklaces, candy rings, or 100 Grand candy bars.

Before your worship service, have a few volunteers perform the publicity skit on pages 130-131. Show the promotional segment of the *Discover!* video again.

Mail additional Treasure Hunt Bible Adventure invitation postcards as necessary.

○ **Make backup and emergency plans.** What if it rains during your program? Plan in advance how you'll handle bad weather. You may also want to line up backup Clue Crew Leaders in case some drop out.

Inform Discovery Site Leaders and Clue Crew Leaders of procedures you'll follow if there's a fire or other emergency.

One Week Before TREASURE HUNT BIBLE ADVENTURE

○ **Dedicate Treasure Hunt Bible Adventure staff.** Introduce Discovery Site Leaders, Clue Crew Leaders, and other volunteers during your church service. Then have your pastor or other church members pray that God will use these workers to touch kids' lives with his love during Treasure Hunt Bible Adventure.

○ **Assign kids to Clue Crews.** Photocopy the "Clue Crew Roster" (p. 148). You'll need one roster for each Clue Crew. Using the preregistration forms you've received, assign children to elementary and preschool Clue Crews. Each Clue Crew should have no more than five children and one adult or teenage Clue Crew Leader. Be sure that each preschool Clue Crew has a mix of three-, four-, and five-year-olds.

Here are some additional guidelines for assigning crews:

- ✔ Fill in the "Clue Crew Roster" (p. 148) in pencil—you'll probably make changes as you work.
- ✔ Whenever possible, place a child from each age level in each Clue Crew. If the age distribution at your program is uneven, include as wide an age range as you can. Avoid forming single-age Clue Crews.
- ✔ If a child is bringing a friend, assign the two children to the same Clue Crew if possible. If a child is bringing several friends, assign pairs of kids to different Clue Crews.
- ✔ In general, it works best to assign siblings to different Clue Crews. However, you know the children in your church. Use your judgment as to whether siblings should be together.
- ✔ If you anticipate behavior problems with certain children or have children with special needs, assign them to Clue Crews that have more experienced adult Clue Crew Leaders.
- ✔ If you have children who are particularly helpful or cooperative, assign them to Clue Crews that have teenage Clue Crew Leaders.

Field Test Findings

We've received countless letters from Group VBS customers who've admitted they were skeptical about forming combined-age crews. But when these customers took a leap of faith and tried combined-age crews, they were amazed at how well they worked! Most people noted a decline in discipline problems, an increase in cooperation, and a special bonding among crew members.

A CLUE FOR YOU!

If you're planning for a family VBS, assign entire families to each Clue Crew. Then, add single adults, grandparents, visiting children, or smaller families to the crews. Remember to leave several Clue Crews open, so you can add new members on opening day!

MAPPING OUT YOUR ADVENTURE

Field Test Findings

In our field test, it worked well to have Clue Crew Leaders arrive at least ten to fifteen minutes early each day. Each crew leader picked up a daily schedule and then waited in his or her crew area in Treasure Hunt Sing & Play. This made it easy for kids to find their crew leaders and settle in right away.

Field Test Findings

The huddle and prayer time proved to be helpful for everyone. For example, when a teenage crew leader shared that she was having trouble with one of her crew members, an older crew leader mentioned that she had a small crew and would be glad to have the two groups combine. Since we caught the situation early, the "combo crew" (and its leaders) had a fantastic week! Also, seeing their leaders pray for them was a great model for children.

✔ If you want your program to have a strong outreach emphasis, limit each Clue Crew to three or four children. Then encourage kids to fill their crews by bringing their friends!

✔ Remember to leave open spaces in a few crews for kids who haven't pre-registered.

✔ After you've assigned elementary children to Clue Crews, assign each crew to one of four larger groups. (Remember, one-fourth of the kids at VBS travel together at a time.) Label these four groups A, B, C, and D—or use your creativity to name them something that fits the rain forest theme, such as Groovy Geckos or Fantastic Frogs. Clue Crews travel with their larger groups as they visit the Discovery Sites each day. For more information about assigning Clue Crews to groups, see page 138.

✔ Once you've finished assigning crews, double-check that you haven't forgotten anyone or double-booked anyone.

○ **Meet with Discovery Site Leaders again.** Check with each site leader to make sure he or she has all the required supplies, and answer any questions he or she may have. Work together to smooth out any last-minute details.

○ **Decide when and where Discovery Site Leaders and Clue Crew Leaders will meet at Treasure Hunt Bible Adventure each day.** It's a good idea to have your staff arrive early on Day 1 to greet children and assist with registration. Be sure each Clue Crew Leader has a large sign with his or her crew number written on it.

○ **Help Discovery Site Leaders decorate their rooms.** Use the decorating ideas found in the decorating brochure and leader manuals, or use the general decorating suggestions in the "Facilities: Turn Your Church Into a Tropical Rain Forest" section of this manual (pp. 56-59) to create a "jungle-y" atmosphere.

During TREASURE HUNT BIBLE ADVENTURE

○ **Meet with Clue Crew Leaders during Treasure Hunt Sing & Play.** Each day the Treasure Hunt Sing & Play Leader will excuse Clue Crew Leaders for a quick huddle and prayer with you outside the Treasure Hunt Sing & Play area. This is a great time to ask crew leaders if they have any needs or concerns, make last-minute announcements or schedule changes, and encourage your crew leaders. Lead a prayer, asking God to bless your day, protect everyone, and give all leaders wisdom as they work with each child.

○ **Register new children.** Make sure you have plenty of workers on hand to register kids the first day! (This is an excellent way to use volunteers who aren't available to help the entire week.) Set up separate registration sites for preregistration check-in and walk-in registration. Follow the Day 1 registration procedures outlined on pages 141-142.

After Day 1, maintain a registration table to register kids who join your program midweek.

○ **Meet with Discovery Site Leaders and Clue Crew Leaders after each day's program.** Check in with all Treasure Hunt Bible Adventure staff to see what went smoothly and what could be improved for future days. Be prepared to change schedules, rooms, or procedures! You may even need to reassign some Clue Crews. Work together to make any necessary changes to ensure that everything runs smoothly.

○ **Give announcements during Treasure Hunt Sing & Play or Treasure Time Finale.** During the course of the program, you may need to change schedules, locations, or Clue Crew assignments. You also may have personal messages or lost-and-found items to deliver to participants. Each day, check with the Treasure Hunt Sing & Play Leader and Treasure Time Finale Leader to schedule any announcements you'd like everyone to hear.

○ **Attend Treasure Hunt Sing & Play and Treasure Time Finale each day.** These opening and closing activities will give you a good indication of how your expedition is proceeding. They also provide opportunities for children to see you and to identify you as the Treasure Hunt Director. On Day 1, you'll announce Clue Crew group assignments (A, B, C, D) and will join other staff members in teaching children the motions to "I've Found Me a Treasure." Each day, the Treasure Hunt Sing & Play Leader may call on you to pray before dismissing kids to their Discovery Sites. Besides, you'll have fun!

○ **Make sure all Discovery Site Leaders and Clue Crew Leaders are present each day.** Arrange for substitutes if necessary. If you're in a pinch for Clue Crew Leaders, ask the Treasure Hunt Sing & Play Leader and Treasure Time Finale Leader to fill in—or appoint yourself crew leader for a day.

○ **Make sure Discovery Site Leaders and Clue Crew Leaders have the supplies they need each day.** Have a runner available to collect or purchase additional supplies if necessary.

○ **Help with discipline problems as necessary.** In Treasure Hunt Bible Adventure field tests (and from real programs across the country!), workers encountered virtually no discipline problems. Each day was so full of fun Bible-learning activities that kids didn't have time to misbehave. Combined-age Clue Crews encourage kids to work together instead of squabble, and minor problems can be handled by Discovery Site Leaders or Clue Crew Leaders.

○ **Stock and maintain a first-aid site.** Keep a good supply of adhesive bandages and first-aid ointment on hand along with phone numbers for local clinics and hospitals. You may also want to keep photocopies of kids' registration forms near your first-aid site. You can use the forms to check for allergies or other health concerns.

○ **Prepare Treasure Hunt Bible Adventure completion certificates**

Field Test Findings

During our field test, we met each afternoon for prayer and lunch and to talk about the highlights of the day. This was a fun time for volunteers to relax and share stories about what had happened during their Discovery Sites or about what the kids in their Clue Crews had done. Not only did we glean important information (to include in the finished program), but it gave everyone a peek at the other exciting things going on at Treasure Hunt Bible Adventure.

Field Test Findings

Midweek, one of our co-directors had the time (and creativity) to create a simple newsletter for parents. She included quotes from kids, a cute poem about what we'd been learning, Operation Kid-to-Kid updates, and other glimpses into the rest of the week. Parents appreciated the update, and it helped them understand what their kids were so excited about!

A Clue for You!

It's important to check your registration forms for any mention of food allergies. Let the Treasure Treats Leader know as soon as possible so he or she can make alternative snacks if necessary.

A Clue for You!

Networking is the way to go! If members of another local church are going to hold Treasure Hunt Bible Adventure, let them know when you'll be taking down your decorations. Most likely, they'll be glad to help—in exchange for any decorations that you're willing to part with! It's a great way to work together, help each other, and build community spirit.

MAPPING OUT YOUR ADVENTURE

for your "explorers." Photocopy and fill out a "You're a Gem!" certificate (p. 177) for each child. A Treasure Hunt Bible Adventure completion certificate is also in the Starter Kit, and additional certificates are available from Group Publishing and your local Christian bookstore.

○ **Send the treasure home!** We've heard it again and again: "My kids can't stop singing those songs!" Well, when those songs include lyrics such as "I stand alone on the Word of God," "Let us pray," or "Oh, how I love Jesus because he first loved me," why would you want kids to stop singing them? Plan to provide (or sell) *Treasure Hunt Sing & Play* audiocassettes or CDs for the kids at your program. Set up a table, complete with information, outside your Treasure Time Finale area. Check out the reduced prices in the attached catalog.

After TREASURE HUNT BIBLE ADVENTURE

○ **Collect reusable leftover supplies.** Store the supplies in your church's supply closet or resource room for use in future VBS programs or other children's ministry events. If you borrowed supplies such as buckets, laundry baskets, or cassette players, return them to their owners.

○ **Send your Operation Kid-to-Kid Bible books to the Kid-to-Kid Send-Off Center.** Place the Spanish translations of the Gospel of John with magnetic bookmarks in a large, sturdy box. Be sure to stuff crumpled newspaper or newsprint in any open areas so the box is packed tightly. Tape the box shut, and then simply affix the mailing label from the Operation Kid-to-Kid brochure in the Starter Kit. International Bible Society will distribute your Spanish Bible books around the world! (For more information, see the "Operation Kid-to-Kid" section on pages 33-39.)

○ **Leave rooms decorated for your next church service.** If outreach was an emphasis during Treasure Hunt Bible Adventure, you'll be pleased when visitors from your VBS program come for church. They'll feel more comfortable returning to a familiar environment. Also, church members will enjoy getting a glimpse of Treasure Hunt Bible Adventure.

○ **Follow up with Treasure Hunt Bible Adventure visitors.** Mail Treasure Hunt Bible Adventure follow-up postcards (available from Group Publishing and your local Christian bookstore). Encourage Clue Crew Leaders to make personal contact with the members of their Clue Crews within two weeks after Treasure Hunt Bible Adventure. Use the additional follow-up ideas on pages 174-175 in this manual.

○ **Report on your program.** During your next worship service, invite Discovery Site Leaders, Clue Crew Leaders, and kids who attended Treasure Hunt Bible Adventure to share their favorite VBS experiences. Encourage kids to display their Craft Cave crafts. You may even want to invite the Treasure Hunt Sing &

Play Leader to lead everyone in singing one or two favorite Treasure Hunt Bible Adventure songs.

○ **Present a slide show or post photos from your program.** Kids (and their parents) love seeing themselves on the "big screen." And colorful photos will bring back memories of a terrific time at Treasure Hunt Bible Adventure.

○ **Meet with your entire Treasure Hunt Bible Adventure staff to evaluate your program.** Celebrate a successful expedition! Make written notes of good ideas that could be used for next year's program. Note any problems that came up and how they were solved. Brainstorm about ways to avoid similar problems in the future. Include notes of how you adapted the Treasure Hunt Bible Adventure materials to fit your church. Record the names of Clue Crew Leaders and Discovery Site Leaders who are interested in helping again next year. (You'll be surprised at the number that will!) Bring the Treasure Hunt Bible Adventure evaluation forms included in this manual (pp. 180-184), and have staff members fill them out.

○ **Thank your staff members for all their hard work.** Photocopy and fill out a "You're a Gem!" certificate (p. 176) for each Discovery Site Leader, Clue Crew Leader, and other volunteers. Or use the Treasure Hunt Bible Adventure thank you cards and certificates available from Group Publishing and your local Christian bookstore. You could even hand out balloons, flowers, or baked goodies to show your appreciation.

○ **Fill out the "Treasure Hunt Bible Adventure Evaluation."** Tear out this evaluation form (p. 183), and fill it out completely. Send your completed form to Group Publishing—no postage is necessary! You may also want to give a copy of the form to your church pastor, Christian education director, children's minister, or VBS committee. This helps us plan for the future!

Field Test Findings

You'll notice that this program doesn't include a closing musical, play, or presentation for children to perform. That's because we believe the purpose of VBS is for children to enjoy and experience God's love—not to perform. Through our field tests, we've watched kids sing praise songs just for the pure joy of singing and worship. We've seen them excitedly experience Bible stories just because God's Word is exciting! When kids are forced to practice songs, memorize lines, or perform for adults, the focus shifts from kids to parents. We encourage you to invite parents to each day's Treasure Time Finale to give them a view of the treasures children are discovering! (If you decide to do a "program," skits and songs are easily adapted from the Treasure Hunt Sing & Play Leader Manual.)

When and Where to Begin YOUR TREASURE HUNT

If your church has put on VBS programs before, you probably have a good idea of the times and settings that work best in your situation. Group's Treasure Hunt Bible Adventure works in just about any setting—midweek clubs, day camps, and traditional five-day settings, for example. Use the suggested times and settings listed below to spark creativity as you plan your Treasure Hunt Bible Adventure program.

Options for TREASURE HUNT BIBLE ADVENTURE Locations

● **Your church:** Many VBS programs are held in local churches. With this approach, you control the facilities, you have many rooms available, and the location is familiar to church members. Plus visitors who come to Treasure Hunt Bible Adventure actually visit your church site.

● **A local park:** Kids love being outdoors, and parks draw children who would not normally attend a VBS program. Check with your local parks and recreation department to see about reserving a park or campground for your Treasure Hunt Bible Adventure. Church, YMCA, and scout camps provide ideal outdoor settings since they usually have electricity available.

● **Inner city:** Turn your Treasure Hunt Bible Adventure program into an inner city outreach opportunity. Invite kids from your church to join inner city kids in an inner city church or neighborhood setting. Even if you use only portions of the Treasure Hunt Bible Adventure materials, you'll guide needy children and their families on a valuable quest for the ultimate treasure!

● **A local school:** Since most schools lie dormant for the majority of the summer, consider using their facilities for your program. If public schools are busy with summer classes, check out Christian school facilities in your area.

Options for TREASURE HUNT BIBLE ADVENTURE Times

● **Weekday mornings:** Many programs are held for five consecutive weekday mornings. Kids have plenty of energy, and the summer sun isn't quite as hot as in the afternoon. For a change of pace, you could even plan to hold a morning program during your students' spring break!

● **Weekday evenings:** Since many church members work during the day, some churches find it easier to staff an evening program. This could be a special program that you hold for five consecutive days, or it could take the place of an existing midweek program. If you hold your Treasure Hunt Bible Adventure program in the evening, you may want to include families. You can offer separate programming for parents and teenagers or include them in Treasure Hunt Bible Adventure as full-fledged participants and Clue Crew Leaders. Church members of all ages will enjoy visiting the Discovery Sites! Each family can form its own Clue Crew, or you can mix families and enlist parents as Clue Crew Leaders. If you invite families, you'll want to provide child care for children younger than three years old.

● **Midweek clubs:** If your church has a midweek club or another weekly children's program, you may want to use the Treasure Hunt Bible Adventure materials for five consecutive weeks. If you use Treasure Hunt Bible Adventure during a regularly scheduled midweek program, you'll probably have Discovery Site Leaders already in place. Just assign Clue Crews and recruit Clue Crew Leaders, and you'll be ready for the adventure of a lifetime!

● **Day camp:** Extend Treasure Hunt Bible Adventure to a half-day day camp for kids in your community. (Again, consider holding your day camp during spring break.) We've provided extra crafts, plenty of games, and lots of upbeat songs to keep children actively learning Bible truths...and having a great time!

● **Sunday mornings:** Hold Treasure Hunt Bible Adventure during your normal Sunday school or children's church time. This is a great change of pace for summer for both kids and children's workers. (Plus, it's a wonderful way for families to participate!)

● **Weekend retreat:** Invite children or whole families to participate in a weekend retreat held at your church or a local camp. Schedule Day 1 activities for Saturday morning, Days 2 and 3 for Saturday afternoon (after lunch), Day 4 for Saturday evening (after dinner), and Day 5 for Sunday morning.

For a Successful Treasure Hunt...

The following tips will help your evening or intergenerational program go smoothly:

● Start early so young children won't get too tired.

● Consider beginning each session with a simple meal. Recruit a kitchen team to organize potlucks or prepare simple meals such as sandwiches or frozen pizzas. If your church has a lawn or grassy area nearby, you may even want to barbecue. Families will enjoy this casual interaction time, and you'll be able to start your program earlier.

● Make sure children who attend without their families have safe transportation to and from Treasure Hunt Bible Adventure. Don't allow children to walk home alone in the dark—even if they live nearby.

● Families come in all shapes and sizes. Be sensitive to single-parent families, childless couples, and children who come alone. You may want to assign family members to separate Clue Crews to avoid drawing attention to family differences.

Have fun as you map out the course that's best for your Treasure Hunt Bible Adventure!

Facilities: Turn Your CHURCH INTO A TROPICAL RAIN FOREST

Atmosphere and environment enhance learning, so decorations are an integral part of Treasure Hunt Bible Adventure. They can set the mood for the week and can get children excited about the treasure of Jesus. Following, you'll find a listing of suggested decorations for Discovery Sites and other church areas. Remember, these are options and aren't necessary for the success of your Treasure Hunt Bible Adventure. If you and others want to go the extra mile, it'll simply enhance the program.

Most decorating items can be found among your church members or can be purchased inexpensively. Have fun! Letting your imagination and creativity go wild, you can create a wild environment! Go for it!

Discovery Site Sign-In

This is your registration area. It will be kids' first impression of Treasure Hunt Bible Adventure. Create mystery and excitement by making it look like the entrance to a jungle! Set the tone with vines, stuffed animals, and foliage.

A CLUE FOR YOU!

VBS Directors continue to amaze us with their creativity, hard work, and incredibly imaginative ideas! If you've trekked ahead of us to transform your facility into an amazing, radical rain forest, we'd love to see how you did it! Please send pictures or videocassettes to: VBS Coordinator at Group Publishing, Inc., P.O. Box 481, Loveland, CO 80539. (Sorry, we can't return them!) Or, post your photos on our Web site (http://www.grouppublishing.com/vbs). This is a great way to share your ideas with others who may be gearing up for the adventure!

MAPPING OUT YOUR ADVENTURE

- **Have costumed staff on hand.** Have volunteers dress up in animal costumes (the Chadder costume is extra fun!), explorers' vests, hiking boots, and other "adventure-wear" to greet and welcome children each day. (You may want to have a man dress in a leather bomber jacket, hat, and tan pants and pose as Indiana Jones!)
- **Surprise kids with an "un-frog-getable" welcome!** Check out your Treasure Hunt Bible Adventure catalog to discover a motion-sensitive frog that

"ribbits" whenever anything crosses its path! What a fun and surprising welcome to your program!

- **Play an audiocassette of rain forest noises.** You'll find 2 minutes of rain forest sounds on the *1999 VBS: Skits & Drama* audiocassette. These sounds of rain, thunder, and animals will add to the excitement! Place an audiocassette player under each registration table and turn up the volume.
- **Cover tables and doors with crinkled-paper treasure maps.** Use the Geoami (found in your Starter Kit) to create fun, ancient-looking treasure maps. Kids will love looking at your "clues"—dotted lines that wind through a jungle of "dangers"—and finding where X marks the spot!
- **Create an exciting entry to the jungle.** Crowd the entryway with foliage (real or artificial); then hang crepe paper streamers from the top of the doorway. Kids will love pushing aside the "vines" to enter Treasure Hunt Bible Adventure!

Jungle Paths

Even your hallways can be eye-catching and exciting! As children travel to their Discovery Sites, they'll feel as if they're really trekking through a rain forest, searching for hidden treasures!

- **Create a dark and mysterious jungle.** To help kids feel as if they're walking in a humid, unexplored rain forest, dim the lights in your hallways or

Field Test Findings

We found some huge plastic bugs we knew kids would love; then we placed the creepy crawlers in the dark cave entrance to Bible Exploration. Kids loved the excitement of crawling over bugs as they made their way to the room! And, at the end of the week, we discovered that all of our bugs were still there! Kids had been respectful and hadn't taken any decorations!

A Clue for You!

Be sure to have your Clue Crew Leaders make poster board or construction paper number signs for each Clue Crew. Post each number on a different pew or row of chairs in Treasure Hunt Sing & Play so Clue Crews know where to sit each day.

replace your regular light bulbs with green light bulbs. Cover the walls with jungle-print cloth, wrapping paper, or even green butcher paper. Add large paper leaves and other foliage. Every few yards, place a humidifier to create jungle steam!

● **Photocopy and cut out the arrows from the back of each of the Discovery Site Leader Manuals.** You'll need at least two arrows per Discovery Site to quickly guide children through your facility. Then photocopy, color, and cut out the Discovery Site signs from the front of each Discovery Site Leader Manual. Hang the posters and arrows so kids can find their way to the correct Discovery Sites.

● **Hang vines and plastic bugs from the ceiling.** Kids love creepy stuff, so gather plastic bugs or make spiders from egg cartons and chenille wire. Then use fishing wire or sewing thread to hang the bugs at differing lengths from the ceiling. To add to the excitement, make the bugs low enough so kids may brush against them as Clue Crews walk by! Yuck!

Discovery Sites

Specific decorating ideas for each Discovery Site are listed in the individual leader manuals. Plus, you'll find a treasure-trove of decorating ideas in the decorating brochure in your Starter Kit can! Use the following ideas to reinforce the jungle theme in all of your Discovery Sites.

● **Create a "jungle scene" in each window.** Use tempera paint to cover windows with green leaves, vines, and animals peeking in (or out). Even if you're not using some classrooms, this is a fun way to communicate your theme to those inside and out!

● **Hang posters of real jungles or animals.** Find posters of rain forests, monkeys, endangered animals, or wildflowers. Look through nature magazines to find such pictures, and then post them everywhere!

● **Let animal "friends" welcome children at every Discovery Site.** Add warmth and friendliness to your Treasure Hunt Bible Adventure by having a large stuffed frog, monkey, bird, lion, leopard, or huge butterfly stand at the door to each Discovery Site. Kids will love greeting the animals, and your simple creations will become beloved mascots! (You may want to ask middle schoolers and teenagers to dress creatively as these animals and roam through the "jungle" each day!)

● **Place trees everywhere!** Collect sturdy, cardboard carpet-roll cores to use as tree trunks. These cores come in approximately twenty-foot lengths, so you'll get several trees from each one! Tape paper palm fronds, leaves, and vines to one end of each trunk; then use packing tape to attach the trees to outside walls. (Packing tape may be too sticky for indoor paint, so be careful what you tape them to indoors.) Set monkeys, birds, or butterflies in your trees for added effect.

● **Create a rain forest canopy!** Tape plastic vines, green crepe paper streamers, and even raffia or rope to the ceiling, allowing them to drape down a little, to create a dense rain forest canopy. You may even want to affix a brown trellis to the ceiling and then weave in real twigs, branches, or vines!

● **Make a jungle hut!** Use large appliance boxes to create simple huts that kids can actually enter. Cut a door and a few windows in each box, drape green

crepe paper streamers in the windows. Bend a large sheet of cardboard in half to make a roof for the hut. Then glue rows of paper-towel tubes to the cardboard to simulate a bamboo roof. Or, glue rows of brown paper grocery sacks to the roof, and then shred the ends to look like dried grasses.

● **Let your imagination run wild!** These ideas are just clues to help you explore the many possibilities. Check out local resources—businesses, libraries, universities, craft and party-supply stores, and video-rental stores—for more ways to turn your facility into Treasure Hunt Bible Adventure.

Supplies: Everything You NEED FOR AN EXCITING EXPEDITION

Here are the supplies you'll need for each Discovery Site. These supply lists are also printed in their respective leader manuals. Note that some supplies can be shared among Discovery Sites.

Treasure Hunt Sing & Play

Things you can find around your home:
○ a Bible

Things you can find around your church:
○ a cassette or CD player
○ an overhead projector (optional)
○ a microphone/sound system

A CLUE FOR YOU!

Many elementary schools do science or social studies units on the rain forest. Ask teachers in your congregation if they have supplies you can borrow, such as posters or other decorating items.

Things you'll need to collect or purchase:
- *Treasure Hunt Sing & Play* audiocassette or CD*
- *1999 VBS: Skits & Drama* audiocassette*
- *Treasure Hunt Sing & Play Transparencies* (optional)
- a bamboo whistle* or other attention-getting signal

*These items are available from Group Publishing and your local Christian bookstore.

A CLUE FOR YOU!

Treasure Hunt Sing & Play music is a great way to help kids remember exciting Bible truths long after VBS. Now, it's even easier (and more affordable) to get this unforgettable music into kids' hands and homes!

If you purchase 20 to 39 copies of the *Treasure Hunt Sing & Play* audiocassette, you'll pay just $4.99 each.

If you purchase 40 to 59 copies, you'll pay just $3.99 each.

If you purchase more than 60 copies, you'll pay just $2.99 each.

IMPORTANT LEGAL INFORMATION

For Your Information...

When you buy a *Treasure Hunt Sing & Play* audiocassette, CD, or song lyrics transparencies, you also buy the right to use the thirteen Treasure Hunt Bible Adventure songs. You're welcome to play these songs as often as you like. But the companies that own these songs haven't given you (or us!) the right to duplicate any *Treasure Hunt Sing & Play* products. Making your own copies—even to use at VBS—is against the law...a fact many people don't know.

Bible Exploration

Things you can find around your home:
- a Bible
- photos of loved ones
- small- to medium-sized cardboard boxes (one or two dozen, depending on how large you build your tomb entrance on Day 4)
- newspapers
- three or four empty cereal boxes (to throw "overboard" on Day 5)
- an audiocassette player
- penlights or small flashlights
- a robe, sash, head scarf, and sandals (for Mary Magdalene's costume)
- a robe, towel, two neckties or ropes, and sandals (for Jesus' costume, white would be best)
- a robe, towel, two neckties or ropes, and sandals (for Habib's costume, worn out clothes are best)
- strips of white cloth (for Jesus' burial clothes)
- paper towels
- several bowls of water
- small bowls or cups
- a small loaf of bread and a cup of grape juice (for the Last Supper)

Things you can find around your church:
- a wide-tipped black marker
- watercolor markers
- pencils
- scissors

Things you'll need to collect or purchase:
- air mattresses, inner tubes, and/or old sofa cushions

- ○ 2x2 pieces of wood or cardboard material to make a 4- to 5-foot boat
- ○ a bamboo whistle* or other attention-getting signal

*These items are available from Group Publishing and your local Christian bookstore.

Craft Cave

Things you can find around your home:
- ○ large, plastic cups
- ○ buckets or bowls
- ○ plastic spoons
- ○ paper towels
- ○ unpopped popcorn
- ○ ¼-cup measuring cups

Things you can find around your church:
- ○ craft sticks
- ○ scissors (Fiskars for Kids work best)
- ○ warm water
- ○ markers or crayons
- ○ transparent tape
- ○ masking tape (optional)
- ○ index cards
- ○ washable markers
- ○ a cassette or CD player (optional)

Things you'll need to collect or purchase:
- ○ liquid starch
- ○ school glue gel
- ○ Jungle Gel Cells*
- ○ Treasure Hunt sticker sheets*
- ○ "Bible Point" posters*
- ○ "Operation Kid-to-Kid" posters*
- ○ Operation Kid-to-Kid Magnetic Bookmarks*
- ○ Elementary Student Books*
- ○ Surprise Treasure Chest Kits*
- ○ Mini Jungle Vines*
- ○ Good News Treasure Pouches*
- ○ one treasure chest or bowl
- ○ Good News beads* (yellow, red, white, green)
- ○ Hershey's Kisses candies
- ○ Rain Forest Creatures*
- ○ a *Treasure Hunt Sing & Play* audiocassette or CD* (optional)
- ○ bamboo whistle* or other attention-getting device

*These items are available from Group Publishing and your local Christian bookstore.

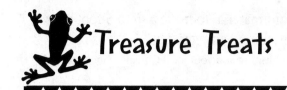

Treasure Treats

FOOD SUPPLIES

	Item	Required Amount	Total Number of Participants	Total Required Amount
DAY 1	cupcakes, baked in cupcake papers	1 per participant	X _____	= _____
	whipped topping	1 tablespoon per participant	X _____	= _____
	candy orange slices	1 per participant	X _____	= _____
	Gummy Bears	1 per participant	X _____	= _____
	blue food coloring			1 small vial
	water	2 quarts for every 10 participants	# of participants ÷ 10 = ___	X 2 = ___ qts.
DAY 2	hot dog buns	½ per participant	X _____	= _____
	strawberry preserves	1 teaspoon per participant	X _____	= _____
	cream cheese	2 teaspoons per participant	X _____	= _____
	strawberries	½ per participant	X _____	= _____
	Pull-n-Peel Twizzlers red licorice	2 strings per participant	X _____	= _____
	juice	2 quarts for every 10 participants	# of participants ÷ 10 = ___	X 2 = ___ qts.
DAY 3	mini pretzel twists	⅛ cup per participant	X _____	= _____
	Goldfish crackers	⅛ cup per participant	X _____	= _____
	M&M's candies	⅛ cup per participant	X _____	= _____
	Gummy Bears	4 to 5 per participant	X _____	= _____
	Honey Nut Cheerios	⅛ cup per participant	X _____	= _____
	Life cereal	⅛ cup per participant	X _____	= _____
	juice	2 quarts for every 10 participants	# of participants ÷ 10 = ___	X 2 = ___ qts.
DAY 4	Sugar cones	1 per participant, plus a few extras to account for breakage	X _____	= _____
	Oreo cookies	1 per participant	X _____	= _____
	pre-made frosting	1 tablespoon per participant	X _____	= _____
	juice	2 quarts for every 10 participants	# of participants ÷ 10 = ___	X 2 = ___ qts.
DAY 5	pita bread	¼ piece per participant	X _____	= _____
	lunch meat	1 slice per participant	X _____	= _____
	cheese slices	½ per participant	X _____	= _____
	large pretzel rods	½ per participant	X _____	= _____
	small pretzel sticks	2 per participant	X _____	= _____
	juice	2 quarts for every 10 participants	# of participants ÷ 10 = ___	X 2 = ___ qts.

MAPPING OUT YOUR ADVENTURE

SERVING SUPPLIES

Item	Required Amount	Total Number of Participants	Total Required Amount
paper cups	6 per participant	X _____	= _____
napkins	6 per participant	X _____	= _____
paper plates	3 per participant	X _____	= _____
plastic knives	2 per Mission Munchies Service Crew	X _____	= _____
shallow bowls or plates	1 per Treasure Treats Service Crew	X _____	= _____
"snackmaker" (plastic food-handler) gloves*	5 per participant	X _____	= _____
pitchers	2 for every 10 participants	X _____	= _____
resealable plastic bags (sandwich size)	3 per Treasure Treats Service Crew	X _____	= _____
paring knife	1 per Treasure Treats Service Crew	X _____	= _____
large serving trays	1 per Treasure Treats Service Crew	X _____	= _____
large tub or pot	1 per Treasure Treats Service Crew	X _____	= _____
large plastic foam cooler	1 for every 50 participants	X _____	= _____
measuring scoop or clean sandbox shovel	1 per foam cooler	X _____	= _____
silver paint pen	1		
black construction paper	5 sheets for every foam cooler	X _____	= _____
aluminum foil	1 small roll for every foam cooler	X _____	= _____
bamboo skewers	5 per foam cooler	X _____	= _____
clear tape	1 dispenser for every foam cooler	X _____	= _____

A CLUE FOR YOU!
Kids will use the items in the shaded section to create a treasure chest on Day 2.

Other Supplies

Things you can find around your church:
- ○ antibacterial soap or individually wrapped hand-wipes
- ○ two or three rolls of paper towels

Things you'll need to collect or purchase:
- ○ *Treasure Hunt Sing & Play* audiocassette (optional)*
- ○ a chef's hat (optional)*
- ○ a bamboo whistle* or other attention-getting signal

*These items are available from Group Publishing and your local Christian bookstore.

MAPPING OUT YOUR ADVENTURE

Jungle Gym Games

Things you can find around your home:
- strips of paper
- empty plastic bowls
- empty plastic milk jugs
- 1 children's wading pool
- 2 laundry baskets
- 2 or 3 large black trash bags
- 1 watch with a second hand
- 1 balloon pump or bicycle pump
- bandannas or other strips of soft cloth
- 1 yellow item to use as a banana
- old towels

Things you can find around your church:
- masking tape or rope
- 1 permanent marker
- heavy tape (such as duct tape)
- transparent tape
- construction paper
- scissors

Things you'll need to collect or purchase:
- large sponge mitts
- a variety of small candies
- paper lunch sacks
- 8- or 9-inch balloons of various colors
- 2-60 balloons*
- neon-colored tennis balls
- Ping-Pong balls
- a bamboo whistle* or another attention-getting device

*These items are available from Group Publishing and your local Christian bookstore.

Chadder's Treasure Hunt Theater

Things you can find around your home:
- a clock or a watch

Things you can find around your church:
- a large color TV
- a VCR
- a cassette player (optional)

Things you'll need to collect or purchase:
- ○ the *Chadder's Treasure Hunt Adventure* video*
- ○ Student Books*
- ○ Treasure Hunt sticker sheets*
- ○ Bible highlighters*
- ○ the *Treasure Hunt Sing & Play* audiocassette* (optional)
- ○ a bamboo whistle* or another attention-getting device

*These items are available from Group Publishing and your local Christian bookstore.

Treasure Time Finale

Things you can find around your home:
- ○ a Bible
- ○ a clock or a watch
- ○ large plastic trash bags
- ○ a straight pin
- ○ a large, clear plastic dropcloth (to cover a carpeted floor)
- ○ a large, unbreakable bowl filled with water
- ○ several towels
- ○ simple costumes for the "Hailing the Chief" skit (some costume possibilities include a wig and a scarf for the woman, a sport coat for the man, headphones for the young man, a bathrobe for the sleepy woman, and a baseball cap and teddy bear for the child)
- ○ two large paper bags
- ○ a simple costume for the character of Jesus (such as a white sheet and a gold cloth strip to tie around the waist)
- ○ string

Things you can find around your church:
- ○ a microphone (if there are more than forty kids or if you're using a large room)
- ○ an audiocassette or CD player
- ○ brightly colored slips of paper cut into various shapes
- ○ slides, a slide projector, and a screen (if you decide to do a slide show)
- ○ poster board
- ○ markers

Things you'll need to collect or purchase:
- ○ Operation Kid-to-Kid posters* from the Craft Cave Leader
- ○ treasure chests
- ○ 9-inch green and blue balloons*
- ○ 15 balloons*
- ○ large plastic jewels*
- ○ heart locks with keys*
- ○ simple magnifying glasses*
- ○ "gold" coins*

○ a chirping parrot*
○ compasses*
○ the *Treasure Hunt Sing & Play* audiocassette or CD (from the Treasure Hunt Sing & Play Leader)
○ the *Skits & Drama* audiocassette*
○ a bamboo whistle* or another attention-getting device

*These items are available from Group Publishing and your local Christian bookstore.

Preschool Bible Treasure Land

Things you can find around your home:

○ a Bible
○ crayons
○ paper towels
○ three bedsheets or towels or other simple supplies for Bible-time costumes
○ a flat bedsheet (preferably blue)
○ five inner tubes or blow-up swim tubes
○ small toys or kitchen items to sink and float
○ three cinder blocks
○ a bath towel
○ a Crock-Pot with savory-smelling contents (optional)
○ a bucket
○ dishwashing soap (Joy liquid works best)
○ plastic wrap
○ wax paper
○ two to four paintbrushes
○ Bubble Wrap scraps
○ two gift-wrapped boxes
○ a mirror
○ a broomstick
○ fabric scraps
○ an old garden hose
○ two funnels
○ spray bottles filled with water
○ blue food coloring
○ facial tissues
○ a plastic outdoor garbage can (clean and disinfected that can be cut apart)
○ a box of cereal

Things you can find around your church:

○ a cassette player
○ masking tape
○ transparent tape
○ paper
○ scissors

- ○ glue sticks
- ○ craft glue
- ○ blocks
- ○ a flashlight
- ○ permanent markers
- ○ paper cups
- ○ craft sticks
- ○ blue finger paint
- ○ balls and other outdoor play equipment
- ○ duct tape
- ○ scented baby lotion
- ○ toy housekeeping items
- ○ baby wipes
- ○ bubble solution
- ○ plastic gloves
- ○ newsprint or butcher paper
- ○ yarn
- ○ black chenille wires
- ○ watercolor markers
- ○ cotton balls

Things you'll need to collect or purchase:

- ○ *Preschool Bible Treasure Land* audiocassette*
- ○ Treasure Hunt Bible Adventure name badges*
- ○ Treasure Hunt sticker sheets: Preschool *
- ○ Preschool Student Books*
- ○ Jungle Gel Cells*
- ○ rain forest seeds*
- ○ Mini Jungle Vine*
- ○ Good News Treasure Pouches*
- ○ 2 children's wading pools
- ○ 3 8-foot two-by-fours
- ○ a 4x8-foot sheet of Masonite or heavy cardboard
- ○ gel glue
- ○ liquid laundry starch
- ○ dark-colored socks (one per child)
- ○ wire clothes hangers
- ○ resealable plastic snack bags (Use Glad bags only—or you'll have lots of leaks!)
- ○ craft foam hearts
- ○ sponge paintbrushes
- ○ red fabric paint or acrylic paint
- ○ white washcloths (one per child)
- ○ Surprise Treasure Chests*
- ○ glue-on gems and sequins
- ○ 2-liter plastic soda bottles (one per child)

○ potting soil
○ Hershey's Kisses candies or gold-wrapped chocolate coins
○ Ping-Pong balls
○ a bamboo whistle* or another attention-getting signal

*These items are available from Group Publishing and your local Christian bookstore.

BONUS IDEA!

This great tip comes from churches that have fine-tuned the art of collecting VBS supplies! It just doesn't get any easier!

1. Photocopy the "We're Collecting Treasures" ticket below on colored paper. Designate a different color paper for each Discovery Site—for example, blue paper for Craft Cave, orange paper for Treasure Treats, and green paper for Preschool Bible Treasure Land.

2. Fill in the information on each ticket. Indicate whether the item needs to be donated (items that will be used up, such as food) or borrowed (items that can be returned, such as sheets or inflatable tubes).

3. Cut apart the tickets, and post them on a bulletin board in a high-traffic area of your church. Make an announcement to inform church members that this is a simple way to help with Treasure Hunt Bible Adventure.

4. As items are delivered to the specified area, sort them by the color of the attached ticket. Just before Treasure Hunt Bible Adventure begins, collect the tickets and sort them into donated and borrowed items.

5. After VBS simply have Discovery Site Leaders retrieve the borrowed items. Match the items with their tickets, and return the items to their owners.

WE'RE COLLECTING TREASURES

Item Needed: _____

Donated   Borrowed

Treasure Hunt Bible Director:
_____

Phone: _____

Your Name: _____

Phone: _____

Please return this item to me by: _____

Please attach this ticket to the item and deliver it to _____ by
_____(date). Thank you.

Permission to photocopy this ticket from Group's Treasure Hunt Bible Adventure: Treasure Hunt Bible Adventure Director Manual granted for local church use. Copyright © Group Publishing, Inc., P.O. Box 481, Loveland, CO 80539.

DAILY SUPPLIES

Many VBS Directors requested a daily supply list, so they could see what days certain supplies were needed. Check out the chart below to see if there are supplies that can be shared between Discovery Sites. Treasure Treats is not included in the

DISCOVERY SITE	SUPPLIES YOU'LL USE EVERY DAY...	DAY 1
TREASURE HUNT SING & PLAY	A Bible, *Treasure Hunt Sing & Play* audiocassette* (optional), an audiocassette or CD player, *1999 VBS: Skits & Drama* audiocassette* (optional), a microphone/sound system, *Treasure Hunt Sing & Play Transparencies** (optional), an overhead projector (optional)	A "treasure map" and binoculars (optional)
CRAFT CAVE	"Bible Point" posters, *Treasure Hunt Sing & Play* audiocassette* (optional), an audiocassette or CD player (optional)	Craft sticks; large, plastic cups; Jungle Gel Cells*; Treasure Hunt sticker sheets*; Mini Jungle Vines*; buckets or bowls; plastic spoons; liquid starch; school glue gel; paper towels
BIBLE EXPLORATION	a Bible	An audiocassette player; a penlight or small flashlight; large cardboard (cut from appliance boxes) or long tables; air mattresses, inner tubes, and/or old sofa cushions and pillows; a large box-type fan; duct tape; clear packing tape; 10x25-foot piece of black plastic; *1999 VBS: Skits & Drama* audiocassette: "Disciples at Sea"*; large plastic garbage bags
JUNGLE GYM GAMES		Large sponge mitts, children's wading pool, water, old towels, masking tape or a rope, 8- or 9-inch balloons, plastic drinking straws, construction paper, scissors
CHADDER'S TREASURE HUNT THEATER	A TV and VCR, *Chadder's Treasure Hunt Adventure* video*, Student Books*, Bible highlighters*, Treasure Hunt sticker sheets*, *Treasure Hunt Sing & Play* audiocassette* (optional), an audiocassette or CD player (optional)	A Student Book from the Starter Kit*, pens or fine-tip markers, masking tape, chalkboard or large sheet of newsprint
TREASURE TIME FINALE	A Bible, a microphone, *Treasure Hunt Sing & Play* audiocassette* (optional), an audiocassette or CD player (optional), a clock or watch, two treasure chests	Nine-inch green and blue balloons*, large plastic trash bags, a straight pin, *Skits & Drama* audiocassette*, large plastic jewels*

chart, due to the specific nature of the food items. Also, check with the Preschool Director to see what supplies he or she will need each day.

DAY 2	DAY 3	DAY 4	DAY 5
A "treasure map," binoculars, and a towel (optional)	Binoculars, a treasure chest, and a yellow bandanna (optional)	A treasure chest, a treasure map, and real or plastic bananas (optional)	A backpack (optional)
Treasure Hunt sticker sheets*, Operation Kid-to-Kid Magnetic Bookmarks*, Elementary Student Books*, "Operation Kid-to-Kid" posters*, markers or crayons	Treasure Hunt sticker sheets*, Surprise Treasure Chest kits*, "Operation Kid-to-Kid" posters*, markers or crayons, transparent tape	Good News Treasure Pouches*, Good News beads*, scissors; "Operation Kid-to-Kid" posters*, transparent tape; Hershey's Kisses candies; a treasure chest or bowl; masking tape, Mini Jungle Vine	Rain Forest Creatures and plugs, washable markers, buckets or bowls, transparent tape, unpopped popcorn, index cards, ¼-cup measuring cups
Bowls of warm water, paper towels, a small plastic pool filled with sand, large plastic garbage bags, a sign that reads "Upper Room," an audiocassette player, a small loaf of bread and grape juice; Skits & Drama audiocassette: "Servant Music"	A suitcase, three or four photos of loved ones, newsprint, watercolor markers, pencils, M&M's non-seasonal candies, small bowls	Robes, sash, head scarf, towel, two neckties or ropes, and sandals for Mary's and Jesus' costumes; three photocopies of "Jesus and Mary's Script" (p. 30 in Bible Exploration Leader Manual); small- to medium-sized cardboard boxes; black plastic; wood or cardboard material; a bamboo whistle*	A robe, towel, two neckties or ropes, and sandals for Habib's costume; two photocopies of "Habib the Prisoner's Script" (p. 35 of the Bible Exploration Leader Manual); two 10x25-foot pieces of black plastic; a large box-type fan; clear packing tape; duct tape; small boxes; a penlight; Skits & Drama audiocassette: "Paul's Shipwreck"*; a bamboo whistle*
A yellow item to use as a banana, yellow beach balls, empty plastic milk jugs, scissors, neon-colored tennis balls, rope or masking tape	A variety of small candies, paper lunch sacks, masking tape or rope, strips of paper, 8- or 9-inch balloons in various bright colors, a permanent marker, Treasure Hunt Sing & Play audiocassette (optional), an audiocassette player (optional)	Large black trash bags, tape, masking tape or rope, a watch with a second hand, balloons, a balloon pump or bicycle pump, 2-60 balloons, bandannas or other strips of soft cloth, plastic eggs	Empty plastic bowls, Ping-Pong balls, water, drinking straws, plastic tubing, heavy tape, beach balls, empty plastic milk jugs, laundry baskets, tennis balls of different colors, scissors, watch with a second hand
	Ink pads, magnifying glasses (optional), an audiocassette or CD of reflective music (optional)	Photocopies of the Chadder's Treasure Hunt Adventure video information letter (p. 33 of the Chadder's Treasure Hunt Theater Leader Manual)	
A large, clear plastic dropcloth; a large, unbreakable bowl filled with water; several towels; heart locks with keys*	Simple costumes for the "Hailing the Chief" skit, Skits & Drama audiocassette*, simple magnifying glasses*	Brightly colored slips of paper, two large paper bags, a simple costume for the character of Jesus, the Skits & Drama audiocassette*, "gold" coins*	Slides, a slide projector, and a screen (optional); poster board; markers; fifteen balloons*; string; a chirping parrot*; the Skits & Drama audiocassette*; compasses*; "Operation Kid-to-Kid" posters* from the Craft Cave Leader; a treasure chest

*These items are available from Group Publishing and your local Christian bookstore.

Daily SCHEDULES

Field Test Findings

We discovered that it's a good idea to arrange your Clue Crews so that you have at least one experienced adult crew leader in each lettered group. Adults can offer encouragement, leadership, or helpful advice to younger crew leaders.

Each day when kids come to Treasure Hunt Bible Adventure, they visit seven Discovery Sites. All Clue Crews visit Treasure Hunt Sing & Play, Treasure Treats, and Treasure Time Finale together. In between these activities, the remaining Discovery Sites run simultaneously. Discovery Site Leaders repeat their activities four times, with a different group of Clue Crews each time. When it's time for groups to move to a new Discovery Site, walk through Treasure Hunt Bible Adventure and blow your bamboo whistle (or use some other attention-getting device). This helps kids, crew leaders, and site leaders stay on schedule.

After you've assigned kids to Clue Crews, you assign Clue Crews to groups. Each group consists of one-fourth of the elementary-age Clue Crews at Treasure Hunt Bible Adventure. To eliminate confusion with Clue Crew numbers, use letters, colors, or creative critters to label these four groups.

For example, if you have sixty kids, you will end up with twelve Clue Crews of five kids. You will then assign the crews to larger groups in this way:

A—crews 1-3 C—crews 7-9
B—crews 4-6 D—crews 10-12

If you have 150 kids, you will end up with thirty Clue Crews of five kids. You will then assign the crews to larger groups in this way:

A—crews 1-7 C—crews 16-22
B—crews 8-15 D—crews 23-30

If you have more than 150 kids, set up double Discovery Sites for Jungle Gym Games, Bible Exploration, Craft Cave, and Chadder's Treasure Hunt Theater. For more information on running double Discovery Sites, see the diagram on page 23.

You'll notice on the "Daily Schedule and Announcements" pages (pp. 76-80) that groups visit the Discovery Sites in a different order each day. This schedule shift provides welcome variety for kids and allows a different group to perform Treasure Treats Service each day. Treasure Treats Service is extremely important to the crews, who get a chance to share the treasure of God's love.

Preschool children will keep the same schedule each day but will perform Treasure Treats Service on Day 1. Preschoolers will leave their room and join older kids for Treasure Hunt Sing & Play and Treasure Time Finale. They view each day's *Chadder's Treasure Hunt Adventure* segment while older kids are enjoying Treasure Treats. All other preschool activities take place in or near the Preschool Bible Treasure Land room.

Use the sample morning and evening schedules (pp. 74-75) to plan your VBS

MAPPING OUT YOUR ADVENTURE

72

times. Then fill in the times on the "Daily Schedule and Announcements: Day 1" (p. 76). Note any announcements you want to pass on to your staff; and then photocopy and distribute the schedule. Don't forget to give copies to the Clue Crew Leaders! Each day before Treasure Hunt Bible Adventure, fill in the appropriate day's schedule with times and announcements.

A CLUE FOR YOU!

Everyone loves a joke, silly anecdote, or comical quote. Consider adding "smile-inducers" to your daily schedules—it's an easy way to create a smiling staff!

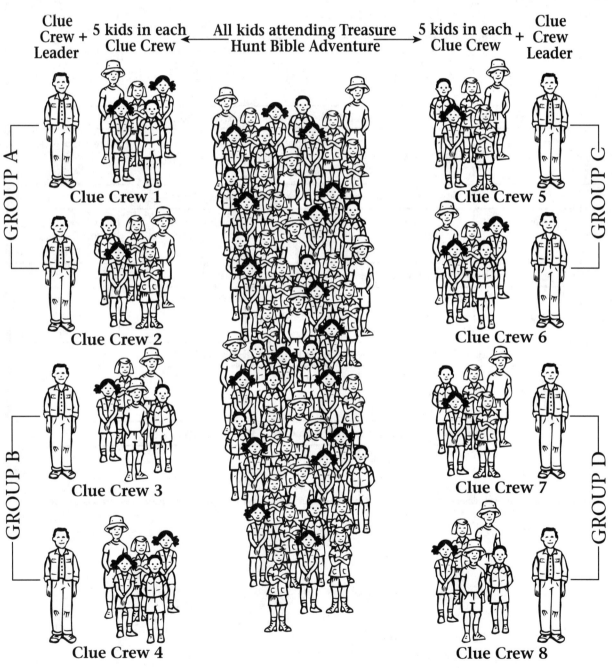

Sample
TREASURE HUNT BIBLE ADVENTURE
Morning Schedule (8:30-11:30)

▼▼▼▼▼▼▼▼ DAILY SCHEDULE ▼▼▼▼▼▼▼▼

Time	Group A Crews 1-5	Group B Crews 6-10	Group C Crews 11-15	Group D Crews 16-20	Preschool
8:30-8:45	Treasure Hunt Sing & Play	Treasure Hunt Sing & Play	Treasure Hunt Sing & Play	Treasure Hunt Sing & Play	Preschool Bible Treasure Land
	\multicolumn{5}{c}{Allow five minutes to search for your next Discovery Site.}	
8:50-9:15	Bible Exploration	Craft Cave	Jungle Gym Games	Chadder's Treasure Hunt Theater	Treasure Treats Service
	\multicolumn{5}{c}{Allow five minutes to search for your next Discovery Site.}	
9:20-9:45	Craft Cave	Jungle Gym Games	Chadder's Treasure Hunt Theater	Bible Exploration	Preschool Bible Treasure Land
	\multicolumn{5}{c}{Allow five minutes to search for your next Discovery Site.}	
9:50-10:05	Treasure Treats	Treasure Treats	Treasure Treats	Treasure Treats	Chadder's Treasure Hunt Theater
	\multicolumn{5}{c}{Allow five minutes to search for your next Discovery Site.}	
10:10-10:35	Jungle Gym Games	Chadder's Treasure Hunt Theater	Bible Exploration	Craft Cave	Preschool Bible Treasure Land
	\multicolumn{5}{c}{Allow five minutes to search for your next Discovery Site.}	
10:40-11:05	Chadder's Treasure Hunt Theater	Bible Exploration	Craft Cave	Jungle Gym Games	Preschool Bible Treasure Land
	\multicolumn{5}{c}{Allow five minutes to search for your next Discovery Site.}	
11:10-11:30	Treasure Time Finale	Treasure Time Finale	Treasure Time Finale	Treasure Time Finale	Treasure Time Finale

MAPPING OUT YOUR ADVENTURE

Sample
TREASURE HUNT BIBLE ADVENTURE
Evening Schedule (6:30-9:10)*

DAILY SCHEDULE

Time	Group A Crews 1-5	Group B Crews 6-10	Group C Crews 11-15	Group D Crews 16-20	Preschool
6:30-6:45	Treasure Hunt Sing & Play	Treasure Hunt Sing & Play	Treasure Hunt Sing & Play	Treasure Hunt Sing & Play	Preschool Bible Treasure Land
	Allow five minutes to search for your next Discovery Site.				
6:50-7:10	Bible Exploration	Craft Cave	Jungle Gym Games	Chadder's Treasure Hunt Theater	Treasure Treats Service
	Allow five minutes to search for your next Discovery Site.				
7:15-7:35	Craft Cave	Jungle Gym Games	Chadder's Treasure Hunt Theater	Bible Exploration	Preschool Bible Treasure Land
	Allow five minutes to search for your next Discovery Site.				
7:40-7:55	Treasure Treats	Treasure Treats	Treasure Treats	Treasure Treats	Chadder's Treasure Hunt Theater
	Allow five minutes to search for your next Discovery Site.				
8:00-8:20	Jungle Gym Games	Chadder's Treasure Hunt Theater	Bible Exploration	Craft Cave	Preschool Bible Treasure Land
	Allow five minutes to search for your next Discovery Site.				
8:25-8:45	Chadder's Treasure Hunt Theater	Bible Exploration	Craft Cave	Jungle Gym Games	Preschool Bible Treasure Land
	Allow five minutes to search for your next Discovery Site.				
8:50-9:10	Treasure Time Finale	Treasure Time Finale	Treasure Time Finale	Treasure Time Finale	Treasure Time Finale

*Kids will need *at least* twenty minutes to complete each Discovery Site. If you need to end your program promptly at 9 p.m., shorten your "search" time to two or three minutes between each Discovery Site.

MAPPING OUT YOUR ADVENTURE

DAY 1

✸ The Bible shows us the way to trust.

Daily Schedule and Announcements

"Do not let your hearts be troubled. Trust in God" (John 14:1a).

▼▼▼▼▼▼ DAILY SCHEDULE ▼▼▼▼▼▼

Time	Group A Crews_____	Group B Crews_____	Group C Crews_____	Group D Crews_____	Preschool
	Treasure Hunt Sing & Play	Treasure Hunt Sing & Play	Treasure Hunt Sing & Play	Treasure Hunt Sing & Play	Preschool Bible Treasure Land
	Allow five minutes to search for your next Discovery Site.				
	Bible Exploration	Craft Cave	Jungle Gym Games	Chadder's Treasure Hunt Theater	Treasure Treats Service
	Allow five minutes to search for your next Discovery Site.				
	Craft Cave	Jungle Gym Games	Chadder's Treasure Hunt Theater	Bible Exploration	Preschool Bible Treasure Land
	Allow five minutes to search for your next Discovery Site.				
	Treasure Treats	Treasure Treats	Treasure Treats	Treasure Treats	Chadder's Treasure Hunt Theater
	Allow five minutes to search for your next Discovery Site.				
	Jungle Gym Games	Chadder's Treasure Hunt Theater	Bible Exploration	Craft Cave	Preschool Bible Treasure Land
	Allow five minutes to search for your next Discovery Site.				
	Chadder's Treasure Hunt Theater	Bible Exploration	Craft Cave	Jungle Gym Games	Preschool Bible Treasure Land
	Allow five minutes to search for your next Discovery Site.				
	Treasure Time Finale	Treasure Time Finale	Treasure Time Finale	Treasure Time Finale	Treasure Time Finale

MAPPING OUT YOUR ADVENTURE

Today's announcements:

DAY 2

✸ The Bible shows us the way to love.

Daily Schedule and Announcements
"A new command I give you: Love one another" (John 13:34a).

DAILY SCHEDULE

Time	Group A Crews_____	Group B Crews_____	Group C Crews_____	Group D Crews_____	Preschool
	Treasure Hunt Sing & Play	Treasure Hunt Sing & Play	Treasure Hunt Sing & Play	Treasure Hunt Sing & Play	Treasure Hunt Sing & Play
	Allow five minutes to search for your next Discovery Site.				
	Bible Exploration	Craft Cave	Treasure Treats Service	Chadder's Treasure Hunt Theater	Preschool Bible Treasure Land
	Allow five minutes to search for your next Discovery Site.				
	Craft Cave	Jungle Gym Games	Chadder's Treasure Hunt Theater	Bible Exploration	Preschool Bible Treasure Land
	Allow five minutes to search for your next Discovery Site.				
	Treasure Treats	Treasure Treats	Treasure Treats	Treasure Treats	Chadder's Treasure Hunt Theater
	Allow five minutes to search for your next Discovery Site.				
	Jungle Gym Games	Chadder's Treasure Hunt Theater	Bible Exploration	Craft Cave	Preschool Bible Treasure Land
	Allow five minutes to search for your next Discovery Site.				
	Chadder's Treasure Hunt Theater	Bible Exploration	Craft Cave	Jungle Gym Games	Preschool Bible Treasure Land
	Allow five minutes to search for your next Discovery Site.				
	Treasure Time Finale	Treasure Time Finale	Treasure Time Finale	Treasure Time Finale	Treasure Time Finale

Today's announcements:

MAPPING OUT YOUR ADVENTURE

Permission to photocopy this schedule from Group's Treasure Hunt Bible Adventure: Treasure Hunt Bible Adventure Director Manual granted for local church use. Copyright © Group Publishing, Inc., P.O. Box 481, Loveland, CO 80539.

DAY 3

The Bible shows us the way to pray.

Daily Schedule and Announcements

"I pray also for those who will believe in me through their message, that they may be one" (John 17:20a-21b).

DAILY SCHEDULE

Time	Group B Crews_______	Group C Crews_______	Group D Crews_______	Group A Crews_______	Preschool
	Treasure Hunt Sing & Play	Treasure Hunt Sing & Play	Treasure Hunt Sing & Play	Treasure Hunt Sing & Play	Treasure Hunt Sing & Play
Allow five minutes to search for your next Discovery Site.					
	Bible Exploration	Craft Cave	Treasure Treats Service	Chadder's Treasure Hunt Theater	Preschool Bible Treasure Land
Allow five minutes to search for your next Discovery Site.					
	Craft Cave	Jungle Gym Games	Chadder's Treasure Hunt Theater	Bible Exploration	Preschool Bible Treasure Land
Allow five minutes to search for your next Discovery Site.					
	Treasure Treats	Treasure Treats	Treasure Treats	Treasure Treats	Chadder's Treasure Hunt Theater
Allow five minutes to search for your next Discovery Site.					
	Jungle Gym Games	Chadder's Treasure Hunt Theater	Bible Exploration	Craft Cave	Preschool Bible Treasure Land
Allow five minutes to search for your next Discovery Site.					
	Chadder's Treasure Hunt Theater	Bible Exploration	Craft Cave	Jungle Gym Games	Preschool Bible Treasure Land
Allow five minutes to search for your next Discovery Site.					
	Treasure Time Finale	Treasure Time Finale	Treasure Time Finale	Treasure Time Finale	Treasure Time Finale

Today's announcements:

TREASURE HUNT™ Bible Adventure

DAY 4

✱ The Bible shows us the way to Jesus.

Daily Schedule and Announcements

"For God so loved the world that he gave his one and only Son, that whoever believes in him shall not perish but have eternal life" (John 3:16).

DAILY SCHEDULE

Time	Group C Crews_____	Group D Crews_____	Group A Crews_____	Group B Crews_____	Preschool
	Treasure Hunt Sing & Play	Treasure Hunt Sing & Play	Treasure Hunt Sing & Play	Treasure Hunt Sing & Play	Treasure Hunt Sing & Play
Allow five minutes to search for your next Discovery Site.					
	Bible Exploration	Craft Cave	Treasure Treats Service	Chadder's Treasure Hunt Theater	Preschool Bible Treasure Land
Allow five minutes to search for your next Discovery Site.					
	Craft Cave	Jungle Gym Games	Chadder's Treasure Hunt Theater	Bible Exploration	Preschool Bible Treasure Land
Allow five minutes to search for your next Discovery Site.					
	Treasure Treats	Treasure Treats	Treasure Treats	Treasure Treats	Chadder's Treasure Hunt Theater
Allow five minutes to search for your next Discovery Site.					
	Jungle Gym Games	Chadder's Treasure Hunt Theater	Bible Exploration	Craft Cave	Preschool Bible Treasure Land
Allow five minutes to search for your next Discovery Site.					
	Chadder's Treasure Hunt Theater	Bible Exploration	Craft Cave	Jungle Gym Games	Preschool Bible Treasure Land
Allow five minutes to search for your next Discovery Site.					
	Treasure Time Finale	Treasure Time Finale	Treasure Time Finale	Treasure Time Finale	Treasure Time Finale

MAPPING OUT YOUR ADVENTURE

Today's announcements:

Permission to photocopy this schedule from Group's Treasure Hunt Bible Adventure: Treasure Hunt Bible Adventure Director Manual granted for local church use. Copyright © Group Publishing, Inc., P.O. Box 481, Loveland, CO 80539.

DAY 5

❂ The Bible shows us the way to live.

Daily Schedule and Announcements

"If you love me, you will obey what I command" (John 14:15).

DAILY SCHEDULE

Time	Group D Crews_____	Group A Crews_____	Group B Crews_____	Group C Crews_____	Preschool
	Treasure Hunt Sing & Play	Treasure Hunt Sing & Play	Treasure Hunt Sing & Play	Treasure Hunt Sing & Play	Treasure Hunt Sing & Play
Allow five minutes to search for your next Discovery Site.					
	Bible Exploration	Craft Cave	Treasure Treats Service	Chadder's Treasure Hunt Theater	Preschool Bible Treasure Land
Allow five minutes to search for your next Discovery Site.					
	Craft Cave	Jungle Gym Games	Chadder's Treasure Hunt Theater	Bible Exploration	Preschool Bible Treasure Land
Allow five minutes to search for your next Discovery Site.					
	Treasure Treats	Treasure Treats	Treasure Treats	Treasure Treats	Chadder's Treasure Hunt Theater
Allow five minutes to search for your next Discovery Site.					
	Jungle Gym Games	Chadder's Treasure Hunt Theater	Bible Exploration	Craft Cave	Preschool Bible Treasure Land
Allow five minutes to search for your next Discovery Site.					
	Chadder's Treasure Hunt Theater	Bible Exploration	Craft Cave	Jungle Gym Games	Preschool Bible Treasure Land
Allow five minutes to search for your next Discovery Site.					
	Treasure Time Finale	Treasure Time Finale	Treasure Time Finale	Treasure Time Finale	Treasure Time Finale

Today's announcements:

TREASURE HUNT Bible Adventure™

Recruiting Discovery SITE LEADERS

Discovery Site Leaders are the backbone of your Treasure Hunt Bible Adventure staff. These are the people who teach and show God's love to the kids who attend your program. Kids look forward to seeing the Discovery Site Leaders each day—and so do you! You need at least eight volunteers—one leader for each of the following Discovery Sites:

- Treasure Hunt Sing & Play
- Craft Cave
- Jungle Gym Games
- Treasure Treats
- Bible Exploration
- Chadder's Treasure Hunt Theater
- Treasure Time Finale
- Preschool Bible Treasure Land

If you're expecting more than 150 kids to attend Treasure Hunt Bible Adventure, you may want to double up on Discovery Site Leaders. Purchase an additional leader manual for each Discovery Site, and run two sessions of each Discovery Site simultaneously. This will help keep Discovery Site group sizes manageable (fewer than thirty kids per session). Or have two Discovery Site Leaders team teach a large group of kids in a larger classroom.

Discovery Site Leaders should be adults or mature older teenagers. You'll find a specific job description for each Discovery Site Leader in the following pages. In general, you should look for Discovery Site Leaders who are

- dependable church members or regular attendees,
- enthusiastic about working with children,
- excited about serving at Treasure Hunt Bible Adventure,
- patient and kind,
- good communicators,
- comfortable speaking in front of groups of thirty or more, and
- gifted in their Discovery Site areas.

Use the details in the following job descriptions to help you enlist leaders for the Discovery Sites. Give each leader a copy of his or her job description, and offer to address any questions or concerns that may arise. Invite Discovery Site Leaders and Clue Crew Leaders to your scheduled leader training.

A CLUE FOR YOU!

If you have enough volunteers, choose two people to team teach each Discovery Site regardless of the size of your program. Discovery Site Leaders benefit from a lighter load and an encouraging partner. Preschool Bible Treasure Land especially benefits from an extra set of helping hands!

A CLUE FOR YOU!

If you want to appoint an Assistant Treasure Hunt Director, ask the Treasure Hunt Sing & Play Leader or the Treasure Time Finale Leader. Because these two leaders present their material only once each day, they'll be free to help you handle last-minute details.

Field Test Findings

Talk about easy recruiting! After our field test, several Discovery Site Leaders volunteered to lead their areas next year! Other churches have reported similar results, with a high volunteer return rate.

List the names, addresses, and phone numbers of your Discovery Site Leaders in the chart below so you're able to quickly access the information.

Once you've enlisted your Discovery Site Leaders, you're ready to begin recruiting Clue Crew Leaders!

DISCOVERY SITE LEADERS

Discovery Site	Leader's Name	Address	Phone Number	Other Notes
Treasure Hunt Sing & Play				
Craft Cave				
Jungle Gym Games				
Treasure Treats				
Bible Exploration				
Chadder's Treasure Hunt Theater				
Treasure Time Finale				
Preschool Bible Treasure Land				

Permission to photocopy this chart from Group's Treasure Hunt Bible Adventure: Treasure Hunt Bible Adventure Director Manual granted for local church use. Copyright © Group Publishing, Inc., P.O. Box 481, Loveland, CO 80539.

Treasure Hunt Bible Adventure Job Description

Treasure Hunt Sing & Play LEADER

Qualifications

You'll be a successful Treasure Hunt Sing & Play Leader if you
- love the Lord and love children,
- have experience leading songs or singing with children,
- can motivate and energize kids, and
- are comfortable speaking in front of large groups.

Responsibilities

As a Treasure Hunt Sing & Play Leader, you'll be responsible for
- attending scheduled leader training,
- repeating the daily Bible Point as you teach,
- learning the music and motions for thirteen Treasure Hunt Bible Adventure songs,
- teaching kids the words and motions to several songs each day,
- leading singing for the entire VBS,
- assisting with Treasure Time Finale programs each day, and
- assisting the Treasure Hunt Bible Adventure Director as needed.

Related Interests

If you enjoy any of the following activities, you'll enjoy leading Treasure Hunt Sing & Play:
- playing a musical instrument,
- directing or singing in your church choir,
- leading worship, and
- acting or drama.

Join TREASURE HUNT BIBLE ADVENTURE:
Where the Bible is the map and Jesus is the treasure!

Permission to photocopy this job description from Group's Treasure Hunt Bible Adventure: Treasure Hunt Bible Adventure Director Manual granted for local church use. Copyright © Group Publishing, Inc., P.O. Box 481, Loveland, CO 80539.

Job Description

Qualifications

You'll be a successful Craft Cave Leader if you
- love the Lord and love children,
- are creative and fun-loving,
- can give clear directions to children, and
- show patience while working with lots of children.

Responsibilities

As a Craft Cave Leader, you'll be responsible for
- attending scheduled leader training meetings,
- collecting necessary supplies,
- preparing sample crafts before Treasure Hunt Bible Adventure,
- explaining and encouraging children to carry out Operation Kid-to-Kid,
- repeating the daily Bible Point as you teach,
- helping children create one-of-a-kind crafts,
- leading four sessions of Craft Cave each day, and
- assisting with Treasure Time Finale as needed.

Related Interests

If you enjoy any of the following activities, you'll enjoy leading Craft Cave:
- science projects,
- missions projects,
- arts and crafts, and
- working with your hands.

Join TREASURE HUNT BIBLE ADVENTURE:
Where the Bible is the map and Jesus is the treasure!

Treasure Hunt Bible Adventure Job Description

Jungle Gym Games LEADER

Qualifications

You'll be a successful Jungle Gym Games Leader if you
- love the Lord and love children;
- enjoy playing games;
- are positive, active, and energetic; and
- can organize and motivate children.

Responsibilities

As a Jungle Gym Games Leader, you'll be responsible for
- attending scheduled leader training,
- repeating the daily Bible Point as you teach,
- collecting necessary supplies for Jungle Gym Games,
- clearly explaining each game,
- leading three sessions of Jungle Gym Games each day,
- assisting with Treasure Treats Service each day, and
- assisting with Treasure Time Finale as needed.

Related Interests

If you enjoy any of the following activities, you'll enjoy leading Jungle Gym Games:
- team sports,
- outdoor recreational activities,
- cheerleading, and
- encouraging others to do their best.

Join **TREASURE HUNT BIBLE ADVENTURE:**
Where the Bible is the map and Jesus is the treasure!

TREASURE HUNT Bible Adventure
Job Description

Treasure Treats LEADER

Qualifications

You'll be a successful Treasure Treats Leader if you
- love the Lord and love children,
- enjoy cooking and food preparation,
- believe children can accomplish big tasks,
- can give clear directions to children, and
- accept and encourage children's abilities.

Responsibilities

As a Treasure Treats Leader, you'll be responsible for
- attending scheduled leader training,
- repeating the daily Bible Point as you teach,
- coordinating food supplies for each day's snack,
- setting up assembly lines to help kids prepare each day's snack,
- serving snacks to the entire Treasure Hunt Bible Adventure,
- cleaning up the Treasure Treats area after snacks are served, and
- assisting with Treasure Time Finale as needed.

Related Interests

If you enjoy any of the following activities, you'll enjoy leading Treasure Treats:
- preparing and serving food,
- maintaining a clean environment,
- working in a kitchen or restaurant, and
- organizing and supervising teams of people.

Join TREASURE HUNT BIBLE ADVENTURE:
Where the Bible is the map and Jesus is the treasure!

Job Description

Bible Exploration LEADER

Qualifications

You'll be a successful Bible Exploration Leader if you
- love the Lord and love children;
- have a flair for drama and can play a role convincingly;
- relish a fast-paced, exciting atmosphere,
- believe in hands-on discovery as a learning technique; and
- feel comfortable facilitating group discussions.

Responsibilities

As a Bible Exploration Leader, you'll be responsible for
- attending scheduled leader training,
- repeating the daily Bible Point as you teach,
- collecting necessary supplies,
- recruiting three to five volunteers to perform simple roles as Bible characters,
- setting up props for Bible Exploration adventures,
- leading four sessions of Bible Exploration each day,
- sharing props with the Treasure Time Finale Leader, and
- assisting with Treasure Time Finale as needed.

Related Interests

If you enjoy any of the following activities, you'll enjoy leading Bible Exploration:
- storytelling,
- acting or drama,
- leading discussions, and
- surprising others.

Join **TREASURE HUNT BIBLE ADVENTURE:**
Where the Bible is the map and Jesus is the treasure!

TREASURE HUNT Bible Adventure
Job Description

Chadder's Treasure Hunt Theater LEADER

Qualifications

You'll be a successful Chadder's Treasure Hunt Theater Leader if you
- love the Lord and love children,
- have an interest in Bible study skills,
- know how to operate your church's TV and VCR,
- understand that videos can be effective learning tools for today's kids,
- enjoy facilitating group discussions, and
- ask questions to help kids connect the Bible Point they've learned in the *Chadder's Treasure Hunt Adventure* video to their everyday lives.

Responsibilities

As a Chadder's Treasure Hunt Theater Leader, you'll be responsible for
- attending scheduled leader training,
- repeating the daily Bible Point as you teach,
- setting up a TV and VCR,
- cuing the *Chadder's Treasure Hunt Adventure* video to each day's segment,
- helping Clue Crew Leaders facilitate group discussions,
- leading four sessions of Chadder's Treasure Hunt Theater each day,
- showing the *Chadder's Treasure Hunt Adventure* video segment to the preschoolers each day, and
- assisting with Treasure Time Finale as needed.

Related Interests

If you enjoy any of the following activities, you'll enjoy leading Chadder's Treasure Hunt Theater:
- watching movies,
- acting or drama,
- leading discussions, and
- have an interest in Bible study skills.

Join **TREASURE HUNT BIBLE ADVENTURE:**
Where the Bible is the map and Jesus is the treasure!

Treasure Time Finale LEADER

Job Description

Qualifications

You'll be a successful Treasure Time Finale Leader if you
- love the Lord and love children,
- enjoy being in front of people,
- are an expressive storyteller,
- like to laugh and have a good sense of humor, and
- can encourage and affirm kids' participation in each day's Treasure Time Finale.

Responsibilities

As a Treasure Time Finale Leader, you'll be responsible for
- attending scheduled leader training,
- repeating the daily Bible Point as you teach,
- collecting necessary supplies,
- distributing each day's Treasure Chest Quest Clues,
- setting up props for each day's Treasure Time Finale,
- practicing each day's Treasure Time Finale script ahead of time,
- recruiting and training other Discovery Site Leaders to assist you,
- leading Treasure Time Finale for the entire Treasure Hunt Bible Adventure each day, and
- assisting the Treasure Hunt Bible Adventure Director as needed.

Related Interests

If you enjoy any of the following activities, you'll enjoy leading Treasure Time Finale:
- public speaking,
- acting or drama,
- storytelling,
- making people laugh, and
- supervising teams of people.

Join **TREASURE HUNT BIBLE ADVENTURE:**
Where the Bible is the map and Jesus is the treasure!

Preschool Bible Treasure Land DIRECTOR

Job Description

Qualifications

You'll be a successful Preschool Bible Treasure Land Director if you
- love the Lord and love children,
- get down on the floor and interact with children at their eye level,
- use simple language that preschoolers can understand, and
- stock your room with blocks, dress-up clothes, modeling dough, and other age-appropriate toys and supplies.

Responsibilities

As a Preschool Bible Treasure Land Director, you'll be responsible for
- attending scheduled leader training,
- repeating the daily Bible Point as you teach,
- collecting necessary supplies,
- leading a team of Clue Crew Leaders for preschoolers,
- telling the daily Bible story in a fun and involving way,
- supervising preschoolers during outdoor activities, and
- leading preschoolers in singing.

Related Interests

If you enjoy any of the following activities, you'll enjoy leading Preschool Bible Treasure Land:
- playing with young children,
- storytelling,
- singing, and
- being outdoors.

Join TREASURE HUNT BIBLE ADVENTURE:
Where the Bible is the map and Jesus is the treasure!

Enlisting CLUE CREW LEADERS

After you've enlisted Discovery Site Leaders, you'll need a group of Clue Crew Leaders. The Clue Crew Leader is an important part of each Clue Crew. Anyone in your church who loves the Lord and loves children can be a Clue Crew Leader! You'll need one Clue Crew Leader for every five elementary-age children.

Clue Crew Leaders don't have to prepare anything; they just come each day and join in the Treasure Hunt Bible Adventure fun. Their week will go more smoothly if you have a brief orientation meeting with your Clue Crew Leaders or if you invite them to your leader training meeting. The *Discover!* video has a special training section that gives them helpful hints on leading discussions and solving any problems that might arise among their crews. We've also included photocopiable handouts that orient Clue Crew Leaders with the teaching style at Treasure Hunt Bible Adventure and give them some ideas for capitalizing on extra time. You can find these handouts in the leader training section of this manual (pp. 113-118).

The following guidelines will help you find top-notch Clue Crew Leaders.

A Clue Crew Leader is
- a friend and a helper.
- someone who offers kids choices.
- someone who asks questions.
- someone who encourages kids.

A Clue Crew Leader isn't
- the boss or the teacher.
- someone who makes all the decisions.
- someone who gives all the answers.
- someone who yells at kids or puts them down.

Photocopy the "Get a Clue! Be a Clue Crew Leader for Treasure Hunt Bible Adventure!" sign (p. 94), and post it in your church lobby. You'll be pleasantly surprised at how many Clue Crew Leaders join your team!

A Clue for You!

If Clue Crew Leaders can't attend the leader training meeting, encourage them to watch the training video and review the handouts from pages 113-118. To allow plenty of time for Clue Crew Leaders to understand their roles, you might consider photocopying the "For Clue Crew Leaders Only" handouts from pp. 113-118 several weeks before Treasure Hunt Bible Adventure. Then staple all the information into a handy packet. Have information packets available at church, or even include the packet in your church bulletin. Your job will be much easier if Clue Crew Leaders read and understand this information well before VBS begins!

GET A CLUE!
Be a Clue Crew Leader for
TREASURE HUNT BIBLE ADVENTURE

Qualifications
- Be at least fourteen years old.
- Love the Lord.
- Love children.
- Like to have fun.

Responsibilities
- Attend a leader training meeting.
- Attend Treasure Hunt Bible Adventure each day.
- Participate in fun activities with a group of three to five elementary-age kids.

IF YOU'RE INTERESTED, SIGN YOUR NAME BELOW OR SEE

_____
Treasure Hunt Bible Adventure Director

TODAY!

Name and phone number   **Name and phone number**

_____   _____
_____   _____
_____   _____
_____   _____
_____   _____
_____   _____
_____   _____

Enlisting Clue Crew Leaders for Preschoolers

Your youngest "explorers" need Clue Crew Leaders, too! Like Clue Crew Leaders for the elementary-age kids, Clue Crew Leaders for preschoolers don't need to prepare anything in advance. In fact, their job is even easier! Instead of leading Clue Crews, Clue Crew Leaders for preschoolers help their Clue Crews follow directions given by the Preschool Bible Treasure Land Director.

Clue Crew Leaders for preschoolers play with children, help them complete art projects, and keep them together when they leave the room. To ensure adequate supervision for the preschoolers who attend your Treasure Hunt Bible Adventure, you need one Clue Crew Leader for every five preschool-age children.

What kind of person would make a good Clue Crew Leader for preschoolers?

A Clue Crew Leader for preschoolers is
- a friend and a helper.
- someone who helps children complete activities.
- someone who gets down on the floor to interact with children.
- someone who encourages children.

A Clue Crew Leader for preschoolers isn't
- the boss or the teacher.
- someone who completes children's activities for them.
- someone who supervises children from a distance.
- someone who yells at children or puts them down.

Photocopy the "Get a Clue! Be a Clue Crew Leader for Preschoolers for Treasure Hunt Bible Adventure!" handout (p. 96), and post it in your church lobby. You'll be pleasantly surprised at how many Clue Crew Leaders for preschoolers join your team!

GET A CLUE!
Be a Clue Crew Leader of Preschoolers for
TREASURE HUNT BIBLE ADVENTURE

Qualifications
- Be at least fourteen years old.
- Love the Lord.
- Love children.
- Like to have fun.

Responsibilities
- Attend a leader training meeting.
- Attend Treasure Hunt Bible Adventure each day.
- Participate in fun activities with a group of three to five preschool-age children.

IF YOU'RE INTERESTED, SIGN YOUR NAME BELOW OR SEE

_____
Treasure Hunt Bible Adventure Director

TODAY!

Name and phone number   **Name and phone number**

_____   _____

_____   _____

_____   _____

_____   _____

_____   _____

_____   _____

Enlisting Treasure Hunt SIGN-IN PERSONNEL AND REGISTRAR

It's important to have staff near the registration tables to greet, welcome, and direct children. You'll also need at least one official Registrar to make sure registration goes smoothly.

For your Registrar, look for someone who
- pays close attention to details,
- is organized,
- is familiar with many kids in your church (this helps when forming Clue Crews and provides kids with a familiar face on Day 1),
- understands the "combined-age" concept, and
- meets deadlines with a cheerful spirit.

Allow the Registrar to read through the registration section of this Treasure Hunt Bible Adventure Director Manual several weeks before Treasure Hunt Bible Adventure is set to begin. Be sure that all registration forms and phone registrations are given to the Registrar.

For Treasure Hunt Sign-In volunteers, look for individuals who
- are friendly and outgoing,
- are comfortable interacting with children, and
- want to help with Treasure Hunt Bible Adventure but can't commit much time.

You can have different Treasure Hunt Sign-In greeters each day—kids will love the surprise! Encourage your greeters to dress up in explorers' vests, Treasure Hunt Bible Adventure staff T-shirts, hiking boots, and tan shorts. Greeters can direct children to Preschool Bible Treasure Land or can help kids find their Clue Crew Leaders.

Field Test Findings

It was wonderful to have a small crew of volunteers devoted to registration! Our directors loved handing that responsibility over to someone else, freeing them up to attend to other details! Teamwork is the way to go!

Be sure to have extra greeters on Day 1 since kids will need a little extra help finding their way.

Enlisting a TREASURE HUNT BIBLE ADVENTURE Photographer

Treasure Hunt Bible Adventure will be a memorable event—one you'll want to capture on film. With today's speedy photo processing, you can make photos a fun part of your Treasure Hunt Bible Adventure program.

Here's how:

1. Enlist a staff Photographer. This person could be
- a parent,
- a church member,
- a friend or acquaintance from your community,
- the Treasure Hunt Sing & Play Leader,
- the Treasure Time Finale Leader,
- your pastor or another church staff person, or
- yourself.

Your Photographer should be familiar with the camera or video equipment he or she will be using.

2. Decide whether you want to shoot slides, prints, or video. The following ideas will help you decide how to incorporate photography into your VBS.

● **Treasure Time Finale slide show**—Have your Photographer visit each Discovery Site and take slide photographs of kids in action. Take the slide film to be processed. On the last day of Treasure Time Finale, show slides you've taken during the week. The Treasure Time Finale Leader Manual suggests ways to incorporate the slide show on Day 5. If your Photographer is fast and if you have one-hour slide processing available, you can even have more than one slide show during the week.

● **Treasure Hunt Bible Adventure photo frames**—During Treasure Treats, have your Photographer take two print photos of each participant (including Clue Crew Leaders) and three print photos of each Clue Crew. (It may take two or three days to complete this project, so start early!) Have the print film processed, and then put the photos in cardboard photo frames to sell or give away as souvenirs. Photo frames with the Treasure Hunt Bible Adventure logo are available from Group Publishing and your local Christian bookstore.

● **Treasure Hunt Bible Adventure video night**—Have your Photographer videotape kids as they visit their Discovery Sites each day. Encourage the Photographer to interview kids about the things they're doing and what they like

Field Test Findings

When we took Clue Crew photos during our field test, the kids came up with a great idea. Several crews had worked before or after Treasure Hunt Bible Adventure to decorate their numbered Clue Crew sign, and they held up their colorful sign for their photo. Not only did the signs add a bright, personal touch to the picture, but they made it easy to figure out which Clue Crew was in the photo!

best. After your program, have a Treasure Hunt Bible Adventure video night where you show the video to kids, parents, and church members.

● **Treasure Hunt Bible Adventure photo display**—Have your Photographer take print photographs of kids in action. Then display the photographs on a poster or bulletin board in your church lobby. This is a great way to give church members a peek into Treasure Hunt Bible Adventure. And extra photos make great outreach tools as an excuse to visit new families who sent their children to Treasure Hunt Bible Adventure.

3. Meet with your Photographer before Treasure Hunt Bible Adventure. Talk about the number and kinds of photos you want. Decide who will have the film processed and who will select the photos or slides you'll use.

4. Watch kids' eyes light up as they see themselves in living color!

Filling Out YOUR STAFF

In addition to Discovery Site Leaders, Clue Crew Leaders, a Photographer, and registration staff, you may want to enlist the following staff members:

● **publicity coordinator**—This person is responsible for coordinating publicity before and during your Treasure Hunt Bible Adventure. This might include selecting publicity supplies, planning outreach publicity campaigns, inviting local TV or newspaper reporters, contacting church and community members, or arranging for community news releases. (TV coverage on Day 5 would be a super way to tell your community about Operation Kid-to-Kid!) The publicity section of this manual will help your publicity coordinator plan a great publicity campaign using the Treasure Hunt Bible Adventure publicity supplies available from Group Publishing and your local Christian bookstore.

● **family resource coordinator**—This person is responsible for collecting the completed order forms and money for family resources, placing the order, and then distributing the items when they arrive. You may want to direct this person to the "Ending the Expedition" section of this manual (pp. 169-184).

● **transportation coordinator**—This person is responsible for coordinating transportation to and from Treasure Hunt Bible Adventure. This might include organizing car pools, planning van or bus routes, or actually picking up children and transporting them to your facility.

● **child-care coordinator**—This person is responsible for providing or

A CLUE FOR YOU!

We've received many letters from VBS Directors who entered a VBS float in a local parade. Consider creating a rain forest float (perhaps pulled by a Jeep), or have an adult wearing the life-sized Chadder Chipmunk costume! What a fun way to alert the community of your Treasure Hunt Bible Adventure!

A Clue for You!

A smooth registration speaks volumes to parents and caregivers who bring their kids to your Treasure Hunt Bible Adventure. A few volunteers who can only commit a little time make a huge difference at your registration area!

coordinating child care for the Treasure Hunt Bible Adventure staff. If possible, child care should be provided for all children (age three and younger) of Discovery Site Leaders and Clue Crew Leaders.

● **registration workers**—You'll need a team of four to five registration workers to ensure smooth, speedy check-in on Day 1. Registration workers check in kids who have preregistered and make sure walk-in participants complete registration forms. With your guidance, registration workers also assign walk-in participants to Clue Crews. Plan to meet with the registration team *before* registration to go over the registration information on pages 133-150.

● **music accompanist**—If you want to use live music during Treasure Hunt Sing & Play, enlist a pianist, guitarist, or even a drummer to help lead singing.

When your staff is complete, your adventure is ready to begin!

LEADER TRAINING

Preparing Your Staff for an AMAZING ADVENTURE!

Using the DISCOVER! VIDEO

Welcome to Treasure Hunt Bible Adventure! We're glad you've chosen Treasure Hunt Bible Adventure for your church's VBS program. We know you're excited about Treasure Hunt Bible Adventure. The *Discover!* video can help you get others in your church excited, too. The video is divided into two segments.

● **The promotional clip** gives a brief introduction to Group's Treasure Hunt Bible Adventure. In this five-minute segment, you discover what makes Treasure Hunt Bible Adventure different from other programs, and you learn how simple it is to turn your church into a rain forest kids will love exploring! Your church leaders, your Christian education board, and your congregation can see kids learning the Bible Points and Bible stories each day. Show the promotional clip in your children's church or Sunday school classes to get kids excited about finding the treasure of Jesus. (This is a great way to get most of your kids preregistered, too!) This short "teaser" will get everyone geared up for the adventure!

● **The overview and training portion** is a great tool for helping volunteers, parents, or other church members understand how Treasure Hunt Bible Adventure works. Your Discovery Site Leaders can be reassured to see kids successfully completing the activities described in their Discovery Site leader manuals. They see kids in a real Treasure Hunt Bible Adventure program enjoying Jungle Gym Games, serving and tasting Treasure Treats, creating spectacular Craft Cave creations, and discovering Bible truths in new and meaningful ways. This twenty-five-minute segment helps Discovery Site Leaders see the "big picture" and become more confident with their roles.

This portion of the video also provides Clue Crew Leaders with valuable information about their role at Treasure Hunt Bible Adventure. Through interviews with real crew leaders from our field test, your volunteers can learn how to work with their Clue Crews, discover what's expected of them, and see the impact they can have on the kids at Treasure Hunt Bible Adventure. Clue Crew Leaders even get tips on handling concerns or difficulties that might arise. Recruiting volunteers has never been simpler!

A CLUE FOR YOU!

The *Discover!* video really does make your job easy! Your staff will love seeing a real Treasure Hunt Bible Adventure in progress, and they'll be reassured that they're activities really *will* be a success. This is a simple way to recruit, train, and prepare your staff.

Field Test Findings

We filmed a group of Clue Crew Leaders moments after each day's program had ended. This format captured the crew leaders' thoughts and feelings right away, and gave us excellent insight as to what activities and experiences had risen to the top. You may want to gather a group of Clue Crew Leaders each day and ask them to give advice to future VBS volunteers. Next year, you'll have an additional training help!

"Gearing Up for the Adventure!" LEADER TRAINING MEETING

A Clue for You!

The *Treasure Hunt Sing & Play Leader Training* video lets volunteers see Treasure Hunt Sing & Play fun in action! This video (available from Group Publishing and your local Christian bookstore) is a super way to add enthusiasm, build confidence, and teach all thirteen Treasure Hunt Bible Adventure songs.

A Clue for You!

Before your meeting, watch the *Discover!* video. Note the places where you'll stop the video to invite teachers to try out actual Treasure Hunt Bible Adventure activities. If your VCR has a counter, you may even want to jot down the counter number of each stopping place in the margin of this manual.

You'll need the following supplies:

Things you can find around your home:
- a Bible
- scissors
- a cassette player
- 2-inch squares of aluminum foil (four squares per participant)

Things you can find around your church:
- name tags
- a TV and a VCR
- chairs
- 2 tables
- paper cups
- juice or water
- plastic knives
- paper plates
- napkins
- markers

Things you'll find in your Starter Kit:
- the *Treasure Hunt Sing & Play* audiocassette
- the Elementary Student Book
- the Preschool Student Book
- the *Discover!* video
- the Surprise Treasure Chest kit
- the Treasure Hunt Bible Adventure leader manuals

Things you'll need to collect or purchase:
- the *Treasure Hunt Sing & Play Leader Training* video* (optional)
- the *Chadder's Treasure Hunt Adventure* video*
- a bamboo whistle* or another attention-getting signal
- Treasure Hunt Bible Adventure staff T-shirts* (optional)
- Clue Crew Leader caps*
- 2 16-ounce packages of softened cream cheese
- strawberry jam
- 2 gallon-sized resealable plastic bags
- hot dog buns (½ per person)
- thin red licorice whips (about six inches per person)
- strawberries (½ berry per person)
- gem*
- heart lock and key*
- magnifying glass*
- gold coins*
- compass*
- 2-foot squares of poster board (one per Clue Crew)
- trash cans
- photocopies of the "For Clue Crew Leaders Only" handouts (pp. 113-118)

*These items are available from Group Publishing and your local Christian bookstore.

Before the meeting, set up a TV and a VCR in your meeting room. Set up chairs facing the TV. In the back of the room, set up two tables. Then decorate your meeting room by draping plastic vines from the ceiling, placing real or plastic plants around the room, and setting stuffed animals in corners or against the walls. You may even want to place masking tape "dashed lines" on the floor to turn your room into a treasure map! To make your meeting room even more "adventurous," try some of the decorating ideas beginning on page 56, or on the decorating brochure in the Starter Kit.

Field Test Findings

When we tried this mixture with strawberry jelly, it turned out slightly gray and a little runny! Yuck! We discovered the importance of using no more than two tablespoons of strawberry jam to create a creamy mixture. If you must use jelly, a few drops of red food coloring turn the gray into a delightful strawberry pink!

Place one package of softened cream cheese in a resealable plastic bag; then add two tablespoons of strawberry jam. Seal the bag securely, being sure to squeeze out as much air as possible. Knead the bag until the contents are thoroughly mixed. Press the mixture into one corner of the bag. Repeat the process with the other package of cream cheese; then place one bag at each table.

Set a stack of paper plates, napkins, cups, juice or water, and one package of hot dog buns at the end of each table, near the cream cheese mixture. Set a bowl of strawberries in the middle of each table and a package of red licorice whips nearby. Be sure to place several plastic knives on the tables and have a few trash cans nearby.

Create an informative "Treasure Hunt Hints" packet for each of your Clue Crew Leaders to keep. Include photocopies of the "For Clue Crew Leaders Only" handouts (pp. 113-118), a sample daily schedule, as well as a list of Discovery Site Leader names. Pass out the packets to your Clue Crew Leaders at the end of the meeting. (You may also want to include the "Helping Children Know Jesus" handout on page 171 of this Director Manual.)

Set a large sheet of poster board under each chair, along with a handful of markers. Then place four 2-inch squares of aluminum foil on each chair. Also place the gem, heart lock and key, magnifying glass, gold coins, and compass inside the Surprise Treasure Chest.

Set out name badges and markers near your entryway.

Play the *Treasure Hunt Sing & Play* audiocassette or CD as volunteers arrive. Greet each Clue Crew Leader or Discovery Site Leader with a warm smile. Encourage each volunteer to create a name tag before sitting down. Thank everyone for coming to this meeting and for helping with Treasure Hunt Bible Adventure.

When everyone has arrived, gradually turn down the volume of the *Treasure Hunt Sing & Play* audiocassette or CD, and then stop the cassette player or CD. Blow your bamboo whistle or use another attention-getting signal. Say: **Let's get ready for the adventure of a lifetime! My name is** [name], **and I'll be your Treasure Hunt Director. It's great to have each one of you as a valuable part of our Treasure Hunt Bible Adventure staff. Let's start our training time with a prayer.**

Pray: **Dear God, thank you for each person here; they're all treasures. Thank you for their willing hearts and their desire to help children find the greatest treasure of all in Jesus. Guide our time together and help us remember the value of each child who will come to our program. In Jesus' name, amen.**

If you're providing attention-getting signals for your Discovery Site Leaders, this would be a good time to distribute them. You can use bamboo whistles, available from Group Publishing and your local Christian bookstore, or any other noisemaker of your choice.

Say: **Today we'll discover some great riches as we dig into our Treasure Hunt Bible Adventure program. Our *Discover!* video will give us a clue about the fun activities mapped out for us at Treasure Hunt Bible Adventure. Before we start the expedition, I'd like you to find a partner sitting near you and introduce yourself. Then take one of the foil squares on your chair, and mold it into a coin. While you do that, talk with your partner about the treasures you hope kids will find during Treasure Hunt Bible Adventure. You have about thirty seconds to share.**

Allow time for partners to share. After thirty seconds, blow your bamboo whistle to regain everyone's attention. Say: **This is my bamboo whistle. I'll blow it whenever I need your attention. I'll also use it each day of our Treasure Hunt Bible Adventure to let you know when it's time to dismiss your kids to their next Discovery Site. Discovery Site Leaders, you may want to use your own bamboo whistles at Treasure Hunt Bible Adventure. Each day is overflowing with activities so you won't want to lose a minute!** Ask:

● **What treasures do you hope kids will find at Treasure Hunt Bible Adventure?**

Take reports from several people, and then continue: **Treasure Hunt Bible Adventure is where the Bible is the map and Jesus is the treasure! And each person here is a valuable part of making that happen. So, turn to another person sitting nearby and give them your coin. Then let that person know that he or she is a priceless part of Treasure Hunt Bible Adventure!**

After a few seconds, say: **Let's begin our *Discover!* video to explore why Treasure Hunt Bible Adventure is such an exciting program.**

Start the *Discover!* video, and show the short promotional clip. Continue into the overview portion of the video.

After the host says, "And crew jobs boost self-esteem as kids discover the riches of God's Word," stop the VCR.

Say: **If you'll be a Clue Crew Leader or Assistant Clue Crew Leader during Treasure Hunt Bible Adventure, please stand.** Invite Clue Crew Leaders to introduce themselves; then give all the Clue Crew Leaders and assistants a round of applause. Continue: **Without Clue Crew Leaders, Treasure Hunt Bible Adventure would remain a buried treasure! We're looking forward to digging into great Bible fun with your help. To prepare you for your expedition, I'm going to give each of you a Clue Crew Leader cap to wear this week. Your caps will help me, the kids, and the Discovery Site Leaders find you more easily.** Give a crew leader cap to each Clue Crew Leader and Assistant Clue Crew Leader.

Continue the video. You'll hear the host talk about Discovery Sites.

After the host says, "Because most Discovery Sites operate simultaneously, you'll prepare just twenty-five minutes of material that you'll present up to four times each day as groups of children explore your Discovery Site," stop the VCR.

Say: **If you'll be a Discovery Site Leader during Treasure Hunt Bible Adventure, please stand up.**

Invite Discovery Site Leaders to introduce themselves and tell which Discovery Site they'll be leading. Say: **Discovery Site Leaders will help guide kids as they investigate the treasures in God's Word. In fact, kids will search God's Word every day as they use their Student Books.** Hold up an Elementary Student Book. Say: **At Treasure Hunt Bible Adventure, elementary kids use an actual Gospel of John to learn how to read, understand, and apply Bible truths to their lives. All kids—elementary and preschool—will use specially designed stickers to mark key passages in their Bibles. After Treasure Hunt Bible Adventure, kids can go back and easily find those verses and apply them to everyday situations.**

Continue the video. You'll hear the host explain how everything at Treasure Hunt Bible Adventure reinforces the Bible Point. Then you'll hear the host talk about Operation Kid-to-Kid.

Stop the VCR after the host says, "They'll discover that sharing God's Word is easy and fun."

Say: **As kids are discovering the treasures in the Bible, they'll be encouraged to share that wealth with others. That's why we're taking**

Field Test Findings

The crew leader caps were a simple way to visually set crew leaders apart from other helpers, "peeking" parents, or Discovery Site Leaders. Plus, we encouraged crew leaders to use their caps as a name tag, by writing their names on the bills of the caps. We discovered that this was an easy way for kids to learn (and remember) their leaders' names.

part in Operation Kid-to-Kid—a hands-on mission project where kids will share the treasure of Jesus with other kids around the world! In each Elementary and Preschool Student Book, you'll find a Spanish translation of the Gospel of John. Open a Student Book and show the Spanish translation. Say: **Kids will be preparing these Bibles for kids in other countries, highlighting verses and adding sticker "clues" to guide Spanish-speaking children to the same treasures they're discovering right here! At the end of the week, we'll present our Spanish Bible books as an offering then send them out for worldwide distribution.**

Let's take a few minutes and see what an impact the kids in our community can have. Under your chair, you'll find a sheet of poster board and a few markers. These are supplies to create the crew signs for elementary crews. They'll help kids know where their crew is gathering during Treasure Hunt Sing & Play and Treasure Time Finale. We'll go around the room and count off, so each person has a number. Write that number really big on one side of your poster board. Make it huge and clear, so kids can see it from a distance. Then take a moment to decorate the sign in a colorful, creative way.

Lead the group in counting off; then allow two minutes for individuals to write their numbers and decorate the crew sign. (You may want to have Discovery Site Leaders decorate their door signs at this time.)

Say: **Now, take a minute and silently pray for the kids in that crew. Pray also for one preschool crew. Ask God to guide their time and to help them discover the treasures in the Bible.**

Pause while volunteers silently pray, and then say: **Amen. Now, gather with three or four others and form a circle.** Pause while volunteers form groups. Say: **Each person in your group represents one elementary or preschool crew of about five kids. Place one of your hands in the middle of the circle to show the five kids you're representing—one for each finger.** Pause, then say: **Each of those fingers also represents one Spanish-speaking child who will receive a Gospel of John, due to our program. In your groups, pray aloud for the children in other countries who will receive God's Word.**

Pause while volunteers pray, then say: **Amen. Go ahead and tuck the crew sign under your chair, and then have a seat. Let's return to our video to discover more about Treasure Hunt Bible Adventure.**

Continue the video. You'll see children making snacks for the entire Treasure Hunt Bible Adventure.

When you hear the Treasure Treats Leader say, "All I have to do is help them," stop the VCR.

Say: **Let's take a break and make one of the snacks kids will make at Treasure Treats. We'll make Love Chests—a snack to remind kids on Day 2 that the Bible shows us the way to love. During Treasure Hunt Bible Adventure, Clue Crew Leaders help with snack preparation by handling sharp knives, pouring juice, and helping kids find jobs they**

A CLUE FOR YOU!

If you'll be focusing Operation Kid-to-Kid in your community, you may want to provide more information on the area where you'll distribute the Spanish translations of the Gospel of John.

A CLUE FOR YOU!

If your entire staff made it to the meeting, pat yourself on the back! Now you have extra hands to create the preschool signs! Preschoolers join Clue Crews that have animal names, rather than numbers. Find the animal clip art on page 124 of this Director Manual, or from the *Treasure Hunt Sing & Play Music and Clip Art CD*. Create large copies of these rain forest animals—such as monkeys, snakes, or birds. Ask several volunteers to glue the animal pictures to sheets of poster board and color them with crayons of markers.

do well. Let's have our Clue Crew Leaders be "drink-pourers" and "strawberry-cutters."

We'll all work in an assembly line to make our treats. Some helpers will cut the hot dog buns in half and place each one on a plate. Then other helpers will squirt a little strawberry filling inside the bun. Clue Crew Leaders will hull the strawberries and cut them in half. Then they'll push half of a strawberry into the cream cheese. Point to the inside of a sample Love Chest. Say: **Notice how the strawberry half looks like a heart? The next helpers will tie two licorice whips around the outside of the bun to make it look like a treasure chest!** Hold up a finished snack so everyone can see how to wrap the licorice. Say: **When we've made a Love Chest and a drink for each person, grab a treat and find a seat near two other people.**

Play the *Treasure Hunt Sing & Play* audiocassette or CD while volunteers create snacks. When everyone is enjoying a snack, say: **Each Love Chest is filled with a heart-shaped treat to remind you of the treasure of God's love. Turn to a partner and tell him or her one way you can demonstrate God's love to a child this week.**

After a minute or two, blow your bamboo whistle and allow a few volunteers to share their responses. Then say: **In Colossians 2:2-3, Paul sums up our purpose in leading kids on Treasure Hunt Bible Adventure. Paul writes, "My purpose is that they may be encouraged in heart and united in love, so that they may have the full riches of complete understanding, in order that they may know the mystery of God, namely, Christ, in whom are hidden all the treasures of wisdom and knowledge." Your loving words and actions are important "clues" that will help kids understand more about God. Let's see what else is in store for us!**

Continue the video. You'll hear about Jungle Gym Games and how they help children remember the daily Point.

Stop the VCR when you hear, "So count me in for next year."

Say: **During Treasure Hunt Bible Adventure, even the games help children discover the treasure of Jesus! When kids work together at Jungle Gym Games, they learn that following God can be wild fun! Let's get up and "monkey around" by trying out one of our Jungle Gym Games! Find three other people and gather with them in the open area in the back of the room.**

When groups are gathered in the back of the room, say: **Take off both shoes and toss them into one huge pile.** Pause while volunteers remove their shoes and toss them into a pile. Continue: **Now, each group will choose a Shoe Sleuth—try saying *that* ten times fast! The Shoe Sleuth will run to the pile and try to**

Field Test Findings

Originally we asked the trainees to simply write the number, without decorating it. But most of them took off and made cool, creative, colorful signs! Several volunteers asked to stay afterward and finish decorating their signs! You'll love seeing how "artsy" this group can be! Plus, your program will look super!

Field Test Findings

This was a great opportunity for adults and teens to start working together as a team. Not only did it allow everyone to get acquainted, (and have lots of fun!) but it was a hands-on example of the way they'd be helping kids in the coming week!

find the shoes that belong to one person in your group. Your group can give silent clues through mouthing words or making motions. Then the Sleuth will run the shoes back to your group and hand them to someone other than the owner. That person must put the shoes on the owner. Finally, someone will need to put the correct shoes on the Sleuth. Ready? Go!

When everyone is wearing shoes, have volunteers return to their seats.

Ask:

● **What was it like to have someone else find your shoes in this game? Explain.** (Humbling, because my shoes are old and dirty; hard because my shoes look like everyone else's.)

● **How did it feel to have someone else put your shoes on your feet for you? Explain.** (Odd, because no one's ever done that for me; strange to have someone serving me that way; embarrassing because my feet were dirty.)

● **What was it like to serve others, either by being a Sleuth or by putting shoes on someone's feet?** (Fun to help out; it was hard to find the right shoes; it felt weird to touch people's feet.)

Say: **During Treasure Hunt Bible Adventure, your kind and loving words and actions will "clue kids in" to what it means to show God's love. You will be a reflection of God's heart. Use another piece of foil to create a heart-shaped coin as a reminder to love the kids in our Clue Crews.** Pause for a few seconds while volunteers make coins. Then say: **Hold your heart-shaped coins and silently pray, asking God to guide your words and actions during VBS. Ask God to lead you to children whose hearts need to feel God's love.**

Pause a moment for silent prayer; then continue.

Say: **Let's learn more about Treasure Hunt Bible Adventure with our *Discover!* video.**

Continue the *Discover!* video and watch as children explore exciting Bible adventures during Bible Exploration.

Stop the VCR when you hear the host say, "You'll find that when you're involved, the kids will follow your lead."

Say: **Participating in each activity is a great way to encourage kids to join in the fun, too. Turn to a partner and tell three ways you can participate during Treasure Hunt Bible Adventure. For example, you could sing and do motions at Treasure Hunt Sing & Play or have fun with Jungle Gym Games. After you've shared, form another foil coin.**

Allow two minutes for partners to share, and then say: **I'd like to hear some of the ideas you came up with.** Allow several people to share, then say: **Your example and enthusiasm are valuable treasures. As kids at Treasure Hunt Bible Adventure follow your lead, they'll discover the joy and fun of following God! Now let's return to our video to see what else is in store for us at Treasure Hunt Bible Adventure.**

Continue the video. You'll hear how fun and easy it is to lead Treasure Hunt Sing & Play, as well as the exciting dramas at the Treasure Time Finale.

A CLUE FOR YOU!

If your Treasure Hunt Sing & Play Leader is willing, this is a good time to have him or her come up and teach the motions and chorus of "I've Found Me a Treasure."

Stop the VCR after you hear the Sing & Play Leader say, "So everybody likes it."

Say: **During Treasure Hunt Bible Adventure, kids will take part in the Treasure Chest Quest. Each day, each Clue Crew will receive three Treasure Chest Quest Clues. Discovery Site Leaders, you may receive a packet of these from the Treasure Time Finale Leader. Clue Crew Leaders, you can work with your crew members and encourage them to solve the clues and guess what's inside the treasure chest at the end of Treasure Time Finale! I'll give you a sneak peek at what riches kids will receive!** Hold up the Surprise Treasure Chest so everyone can see the gem, heart lock and key, magnifying glass, gold coins, and compass inside.

Continue the video to see and hear more about Craft Cave. You'll learn about unforgettable crafts, such as Jungle Gel, Surprise Treasure Chests, and Rain Forest Creatures! Then you'll hear about Chadder's Treasure Hunt Theater and discover how preschoolers will be involved in the Treasure Hunt Bible Adventure.

Stop the VCR after you hear the host say, "And we've worked out all the bugs so the snacks are easy to prepare…even for small hands."

Say: **As you can tell, everyone is on the move at Treasure Hunt Bible Adventure! So children (and Clue Crew Leaders) will enjoy some downtime while they watch *Chadder's Treasure Hunt Adventure*. Let's have a little preview of one of Chadder's adventures.**

Play the first five minutes of the *Chadder's Treasure Hunt Adventure* video to give everyone a taste of what's in store. Then stop the VCR, eject the cassette, and give it to the Chadder's Treasure Hunt Theater Leader. Say: **Chadder has an amazing way of reaching everyone—from preschoolers to elementary kids—and helping them apply the Bible Point to everyday life.**

Hold up a handful of foil coins, and say: **The Discovery Sites you've just seen will be priceless jewels that help children follow God's Word to discover Jesus. Every treasure hunt is an adventure, and every adventure has the element of the unexpected! Get together with a person sitting near you. Think of three unexpected problems that might arise during the week. Then create another foil coin.**

Allow a moment for pairs to brainstorm, and then ask: **What are some of the twists and turns that might happen this week?** Take a few responses, then say: **Although we might see those things as problems, God can turn any situation into something valuable.** Suggest simple solutions to the "twists and turns" mentioned. Then say: **Let's offer our concerns to God.**

Pray: **Dear God, we know that you are in charge at Treasure Hunt Bible Adventure. You've chosen certain children to come and will allow certain situations to arise. Guide us as we deal with your children. Help us to see them with your eyes and to love them with your heart. Use us to display your love in any situation. In Jesus' name, amen.**

Continue the video. You'll hear about what a Clue Crew Leader is and isn't, and you'll hear how Clue Crew Leaders in a real Treasure Hunt Bible Adventure program solved difficulties within their Clue Crews. When the tape is over, stop the VCR.

Say: **Well, I've mapped out our course. Are you ready to dig in and

Field Test Findings

Our treasure chest was absolutely overflowing! It was a cool visual reminder of the way God uses our little bit to do great things.

A Clue For You!

The treasure chest and foil coins make an excellent decoration for your registration table, the Sing & Play stage, or the Treasure Treats table!

A Clue For You!

You may want to photocopy the age-level information sheets (on page 25 of this manual and page 18 of the Preschool Bible Treasure Land Director Manual) to add to your Clue Crew Leader packets.

---

find the treasure? Hold up a few foil coins. Say: **Look at all the riches you've already found! Hold all your foil coins in your hands while I read a passage from Matthew 6:19-21. Jesus says, "Do not store up for yourselves treasures on earth, where moth and rust destroy, and where thieves break in and steal. But store up for yourselves treasures in heaven, where moth and rust do not destroy, and where thieves do not break in and steal. For where your treasure is, there your heart will be also."**

In volunteering for Treasure Hunt Bible Adventure, you've shown that you value children. And because you value children, the kids in our community will discover the overabundance of treasures in God's Word. To show you what I mean, I'll pass around this treasure box. Just as each person here is giving valuable time and energy to children, place your "valuable" coins in the chest.

Pass the Surprise Treasure Chest around the room. You may want to play "Oh, How I Love Jesus" from the *Treasure Hunt Sing & Play* cassette or CD. When everyone has added his or her coins, hold up the chest and show how it's overflowing with treasures.

Pray: **Dear God, thank you for the volunteers you've brought here. Thank you that they treasure children, just as you do. Bless our week at Treasure Hunt Bible Adventure. Give us energy and love that will guide children to discovering the greatest treasure of all in Jesus. Amen.**

Distribute the leader manuals to the Discovery Site Leaders, and Clue Crew Leader information packets to Clue Crew Leaders as they leave. Remind Clue Crew Leaders to wear their caps to registration. If you purchased Treasure Hunt Bible Adventure staff T-shirts for your Discovery Site Leaders, hand them out with the leader manuals.

While your Treasure Hunt Bible Adventure crew is assembled, it's a good idea to take care of lots of "housekeeping" items. You might want to use the clip art on page 124 (or on the *Treasure Hunt Sing & Play Music & Clip Art CD*) to create a "Treasure Hunt Tips" handout. Be sure to include the following:

○ Tell your staff what time to arrive on the first day and where to meet. If you're planning to have staff devotions, let your staff know so they can arrive early. Be sure they know meeting times and places each day after that, as well.

○ Distribute a map that shows where each Discovery Site will be (the *Treasure Hunt Sing & Play Music & Clip Art CD* contains spectacular clip art to help you create a map.)

○ Give a complete list of names and phone numbers of Discovery Site Leaders, registration staff, and VBS Director(s).

○ Inform Discovery Site Leaders and Clue Crew Leaders of procedures you'll follow if there's a fire or another emergency.

FOR CLUE CREW LEADERS ONLY

 ## What's a Clue Crew Leader?

If you've been asked to be a Clue Crew Leader, you've met two important qualifications: You love the Lord, and you love kids.

During Treasure Hunt Bible Adventure, you'll visit different Discovery Sites with a group of three to five kids. **You're not in charge of preparing or teaching activities—you just get to be there and enjoy them as part of your Clue Crew!**

The following guidelines will help you be a "gem" of a Clue Crew Leader!

A Clue Crew Leader is
- a friend and a helper.
- someone who offers kids choices.
- someone who asks questions.
- someone who encourages kids.

A Clue Crew Leader isn't
- the boss or the teacher.
- someone who makes all the decisions.
- someone who gives all the answers.
- someone who yells at kids or puts them down.

 **When talking with kids,**

say,
- Let's keep moving so we can do as many fun activities as possible.
- Listen carefully so you'll know what to do next.
- Stay with the Clue Crew; we need your help in this activity!
- That's a unique way of doing things! How did you think of that? Let's try it this way.
- It's important that we all follow the instructions and work together as a team.
- Please move over here so you can see better.

don't say,
- Stop talking and get back to work.
- Be quiet and listen!
- Don't run around the room.
- You're doing it wrong!
- Don't do that!
- Stay out of that area!

FOR CLUE CREW LEADERS ONLY

Most of the time, things will go really smoothly for your Clue Crew, but every once in a while, you may run into a dilemma. Here's some advice on how to handle different challenges.

If My Crew Won't Stay Together

Encourage your Clue Keeper to come up with creative ways to travel. Build excitement by saying, "Our Clue Keeper came up with a really cool way to get to the next Discovery Site! Let's see if we can get there quickly while we do this."

Encourage Clue Crew spirit by working with your Cheerleader to come up with cheers to say as you travel.

If Older Kids Complain About Being With Younger Ones

Highlight their helping role. Encourage them to help younger kids with crafts and other activities. Acknowledge them by telling younger kids, "[Name of older child] is really good at that. Why don't you ask him (or her) to help?"

If I Have a Clique in My Crew

Cliques can make the Clue Crew experience unhappy for the outsiders. Encourage friendships between all crew members by pairing kids with partners they don't know very well during games and crafts.

If a Crew Member Won't Participate

Help shy children feel welcome by calling them by name often and asking them questions directly. Respond to their questions with a smile and an encouraging statement such as "That's really interesting," or "Wow! I bet that made you feel special!" Also, try giving children special jobs. For example, assign them the task of finding a place for your crew to sit at each Discovery Site.

If someone doesn't want to participate in Jungle Gym Games, that's OK. Treasure Hunt Bible Adventure can be tiring! Let children rest until they're ready to participate. Chances are, when kids see how much fun everyone else is having, they'll want to join in, too.

If People in My Crew Don't Get Along

Quietly take the children aside. Tell them you've noticed they're not getting along. Let them know that although they don't have to be best friends, they do have to be together all week, so things will be a lot more fun if they can at least be kind to one another. (Use the daily Bible Points for these teachable moments!)

If I Have an Overly Active Child

Pair this child up with yourself during partner activities, and suggest that he or she sit with you during quiet times. Try to make sitting still a game by saying, "Let's see how long you can sit still without interrupting. I'm timing you. Ready? Go!"

If the child is really uncontrollable, ask your director if you could have an Assistant Clue Crew Leader.

With a little patience and humor, you and your Clue Crew can have a valuable experience at Treasure Hunt Bible Adventure!

FOR CLUE CREW LEADERS ONLY

Who's Who in the Clue Crew?

During their first Treasure Hunt Sing & Play session, kids will choose Clue Crew jobs and will place job stickers (from the Treasure Hunt sticker sheets) on their name badges. Each child will have one of the jobs listed in the chart below.

- If your crew has fewer than five kids, some kids may have more than one job.
- If your crew has more than five kids, let kids share jobs.
- If children can't agree on who should perform each job, tell them that everyone will get a chance to do all the jobs. Assign kids jobs for Day 1; then rotate jobs each day so that by the end of the week, all children in the crew have had an opportunity to do each job. Kids can simply affix a different job sticker to their name badges each day.

Kids are excited about having special jobs! Encourage them to fulfill their roles, and provide lots of opportunities for them to do so.

Reader		• likes to read • reads Bible passages aloud
Clue Keeper		• collects the Treasure Chest Quest Clues • chooses action ideas for traveling between Discovery Sites (shuffling, skipping, hopping, galloping, or marching) • serves as line leader to guide crew through daily schedule
Materials Manager		• likes to pass out and collect supplies • carries Clue Crew treasure bag • passes out and collects Craft Cave materials • passes out Student Books
Cheerleader		• likes to smile and make people happy • makes sure people use kind words and actions • leads group in cheering for others during Jungle Gym Games
Prayer Person		• likes to pray and isn't afraid to pray aloud • makes sure the crew takes time to pray each day • leads or opens prayer times

FOR CLUE CREW LEADERS ONLY

What Do Clue Crew Leaders Do at Each Discovery Site?

Treasure Hunt Sing & Play is where kids warm up for the day by singing upbeat action songs. Your job at Treasure Hunt Sing & Play is to
- arrive a few minutes early;
- greet your crew members in your designated seating area;
- follow the motions and sing out loud; and
- remember that if you get involved, the kids will too!

Bible Exploration is where kids hear the Bible story. Your job at Bible Exploration is to
- line up with your crew outside the door,
- ask how crew leaders should help out that day,
- keep your crew together until you receive other directions, and
- encourage crew members to participate.

Craft Cave is where kids make cool crafts and learn about Operation Kid-to-Kid. Your job at Craft Cave is to
- listen carefully to the instructions because you will most likely need to repeat them for some members of your crew,
- help kids make their crafts (*when* they need help), and
- help clean up your area before leaving.

Jungle Gym Games is where kids play team-building games. Your job at Jungle Gym Games is to
- listen carefully to the instructions so you can help your crew members follow them,
- perform any tasks the games leader assigns to you, and
- participate in each activity and cheer on your crew members as they participate!

Treasure Treats is where crews come for a tasty snack. Your job at Treasure Treats is to
- gather your crew in a designated area,
- quiet kids and help them focus on the Treasure Treats Leader as he or she explains the snack,
- talk with kids about their experiences at VBS that day, and
- help kids clean up your area before leaving.

Chadder's Treasure Hunt Theater is where children watch *Chadder's Treasure Hunt Adventure*. Your job at Chadder's Treasure Hunt Theater is to
- encourage kids to sit still and listen to the video,
- lead your crew in participating in the activities after the video,
- lead kids in discussion when it's called for, and
- help kids find and mark Bible verses.

Treasure Time Finale is an exciting review of the day's lesson. Your role at Treasure Time Finale is to
- lead kids to your assigned seating area,
- participate in singing and other activities,
- remind your crew to participate without being rowdy or disruptive,
- make sure each child leaves with his or her craft, and
- collect kids' name badges as they leave and store them in your Clue Crew treasure bag.

FOR CLUE CREW LEADERS OF PRESCHOOLERS ONLY

 ## What's a Clue Crew Leader of Preschoolers?

If you've been asked to be a Clue Crew Leader for preschoolers, you've met two important qualifications: You love the Lord, and you love kids.

During Treasure Hunt Bible Adventure, you'll visit different Discovery Sites with a group of three to five kids. **You're not in charge of preparing or teaching activities—you just get to be there and enjoy them as part of your Clue Crew!**

The following guidelines will help you be a "gem" of a Clue Crew Leader!

A Clue Crew Leader for preschoolers is
- a friend and helper.
- someone who helps children complete activities.
- someone who gets down on the floor to interact with children.
- someone who encourages kids.

A Clue Crew Leader for preschoolers isn't
- the boss or the teacher.
- someone who completes children's activities for them.
- someone who supervises children from a distance.
- someone who yells at kids or puts them down.

During Treasure Hunt Bible Adventure, you'll shepherd a group of up to five preschool children. Your role is to love, encourage, and enjoy the children in your crew. If you've never worked with preschoolers before, the following tips will help you.

- Learn the names of the children in your crew. Call children by name often.
- You'll have three-, four-, and five-year-olds in your Clue Crew. You'll probably notice big differences in motor skills (such as cutting and coloring) between older and younger children. Help children work at their own pace, and encourage five-year-olds to help younger children when possible.
- Look into preschoolers' eyes when you speak to them. You may need to kneel or sit on the floor to do this.
- Empower children by offering them choices. Ask, "Would you like to make a Jungle Gel Cell or play with blocks?" Don't ask "What do you want to do?" or children may decide they want to do an activity that's unavailable or inappropriate.

FOR CLUE CREW LEADERS OF PRESCHOOLERS ONLY

As a Clue Crew Leader for Preschoolers, You'll Be Expected to

- arrive at least ten minutes early each day. Report to the Preschool Bible Treasure Land area (Day 1) or the Treasure Hunt Sing & Play area (Days 2 through 5), and be ready to greet children who arrive early. Your welcoming presence will bring smiles to anxious faces!

- greet each child by name and with a warm smile. Help children put on their name badges each day.

- keep track of your crew members' Student Books. Store these in a Clue Crew treasure bag, and place the treasure bag in a convenient location in your classroom or church.

- sit with the children in your crew during group activities such as Bible Story Search Party and Story Surprise Sing-Along.

- accompany children to Rain Forest Discovery Stations. Read the instructions at each station, and help children complete the activities. Distribute supplies from the children's books or sticker sheets as needed.

- repeat the daily Bible Point often. The more children hear or say the Bible Point, the more likely they are to remember it and apply it to their lives.

- always check to make sure all children are accounted for before leaving the Treasure Land! Be sure children hold hands or a rope as you travel.

Never grab, pinch, or pull children as you travel. If a child lags behind, remind him or her to stay with the crew. You may want to walk behind your crew so you can keep all the children in view and avoid traveling too fast.

- report any potential discipline problems to the Treasure Land Director. He or she will help you handle problems appropriately.

- sit with your crew during Treasure Time Finale. Help children participate in each day's show.

- collect children's name badges after each day's Treasure Time Finale.

- help children collect their Student Book Activity Pages and crafts before they leave.

- release children only to a designated parent or caregiver. If an unfamiliar adult comes to pick up a child, refer the adult to the Treasure Land Director.

- assist the Treasure Land Director with cleanup and preparation for your next meeting.

Thanks for joining the Treasure Hunt Bible Adventure crew!

PUBLICITY

Getting Your CHURCH AND COMMUNITY "CLUED IN"

Promoting TREASURE HUNT BIBLE ADVENTURE in Your Church and Community

You've planned, prepared, recruited, and trained. You've assembled an all-star staff for your Treasure Hunt Bible Adventure program. Now it's time to promote your program. Use the publicity items described below to get parents and kids in your church and your community "clued in" to the fun that awaits them at Treasure Hunt Bible Adventure!

In this section of your Treasure Hunt Bible Adventure Director Manual, you'll find the following resources:

● **Treasure Hunt Bible Adventure clip art**—Use the photocopiable clip art on page 124 to create your own custom promotional materials. You can make your own letterhead, memos, transparencies, and more!

● **Treasure Hunt Bible Adventure bulletin inserts**—Distribute information to everyone who attends your church. Just tear out the bulletin inserts on page 125, type in your church's information, photocopy the inserts, and slip the copies into your church bulletins. To help you conserve paper, we've included two bulletin inserts on a single page.

● **Treasure Hunt Bible Adventure table tent**—Photocopy the handout on page 126, and fold the page in half to use as a flier or bulletin insert. Kids can color the handout, cut around the lizard and frog on the dotted line, and then fold the handout up to make it stand up on a table. These table tents will remind all family members of the fun that awaits them at Treasure Hunt Bible Adventure.

● **Invitation to parents**—Fill in your church's information; then photocopy and mail the parent letter on page 127. If you want to personalize the letter, make any desired changes, and then transfer the letter to your church's letterhead. You can mail the letter to parents in your church or your community.

● **News release**—Adapt the news release on page 128 to fit your church's program. Then submit typed, double-spaced copies to local newspapers, radio stations, and TV stations.

● **Community flier**—Photocopy the flier on page 129, and post copies in local libraries, restaurants, grocery stores, self-service laundries, parks, recreation centers, banks, shopping malls, and schools. Be sure to get permission before posting the fliers. You may also want to check with church members who own

A CLUE FOR YOU!

Thanks to technology, you'll find much more clip art on the *Treasure Hunt Sing & Play Music & Clip Art CD*. Use your computer expertise or involve a volunteer computer whiz to help you create dazzling publicity items or jazz up your church's web site.

121

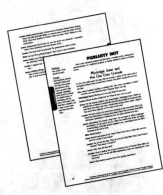

A CLUE FOR YOU!

We've received lots of letters from VBS Directors who discovered the fun of the full-size Chadder costume! They've used Chadder to make surprise guest appearances in Sunday school classes and midweek programs, or to have him help preregister kids! It really helps the excitement grow!

businesses in your community. They may be willing to post fliers at their businesses—and they may even suggest additional business owners you can contact.

● **Publicity skit**—Ask for volunteers to perform this skit (pp. 130-131) for your church congregation. The skit will give everyone a preview of the fun and excitement they can be a part of at Treasure Hunt Bible Adventure.

The following items are also available to help you publicize your Treasure Hunt Bible Adventure. Refer to your Treasure Hunt Bible Adventure catalog for illustrations and prices.

● *Discover!* **video**—You may have already previewed this video when you examined your Treasure Hunt Bible Adventure Starter Kit. In addition to being a great leader training resource, *Discover!* provides you with a "teaser" to show to your congregation. This short video clip gives church members a sneak peek at colorful Craft Cave, marvelous Treasure Treats, and exciting Bible learning that will take place at Treasure Hunt Bible Adventure! Plus the video explains more about Operation Kid-to-Kid, the exciting mission project your kids will take part in.

● **Treasure Hunt Bible Adventure T-shirts**—Invite Treasure Hunt Bible Adventure staff members to wear their leader T-shirts to church events in the weeks preceding your program.

You may also want to purchase a few children's theme T-shirts or iron-on transfers ahead of time and encourage children to wear them at school or in their neighborhoods.

● *Treasure Hunt Bible Adventure* **audiocassette or CD**—Get kids excited about Treasure Hunt Bible Adventure! Play Treasure Hunt Bible Adventure songs in your Sunday school classes or your other children's ministry programs.

● **Chadder Chipmunk plush puppet**—Invite this furry friend to visit your Sunday school classes—or even to make an appearance during adult worship. Chadder Chipmunk can announce the dates and times for your program. You can even ask Discovery Site Leaders to use Chadder to demonstrate Treasure Hunt Bible Adventure activities—Chadder popping out of a Surprise Treasure Chest…Chadder sampling Treasure Treats…Chadder trying to read his Spanish-translation of the Gospel of John…the possibilities are as unlimited as your imagination!

● **Pattern for a full-size Chadder Chipmunk costume**—Ask a seamstress or tailor in your congregation to sew this larger-than-life Chadder costume. Then have a volunteer play Chadder all week long. Kids will love seeing their fuzzy friend before Sunday school, at midweek programs, or at other children's ministry events—and they'll be sure to register ASAP!

● **Treasure Hunt Bible Adventure invitation postcards**—Kids won't soon forget this fun mask postcard that really gets them "into" their roles! Send personalized invitations to all the families in your church and your community. Just fill in the time, date, and location of your Treasure Hunt Bible Adventure program, and drop these postcards in the mail or hand them out at children's ministry

events. These colorful postcards are available in packages of fifty.

● **Treasure Hunt Bible Adventure posters**—Hang these attractive posters on church or community bulletin boards to publicize your program. Be sure to include the name and phone number of someone to contact for more information.

If you're hanging a poster in your church, surround it with photographs from last year's program. When parents and kids remember the fun they had last year, they'll be eager to come back for even more Bible-learning fun at Treasure Hunt Bible Adventure.

● **Giant outdoor theme banner**—Announce Treasure Hunt Bible Adventure to your entire neighborhood by hanging this durable, weatherproof banner outside your church. If parents are looking for summer activities for their kids, they'll know right away that your church has a program to meet their needs.

● **Treasure Hunt Bible Adventure doorknob danglers**— Hand-deliver information about Treasure Hunt Bible Adventure to families in your community with these bright, lively doorknob danglers.

Choose the items you think will work best in your church and community. Then promote your Treasure Hunt Bible Adventure program until you're ready to start the expedition!

Field Test Findings

The co-director of our field test created an eye-catching, interest-grabbing bulletin board. She covered the bulletin board with rain forest wrapping paper then slipped into Sunday school classes to snap pictures of kids. Next, she cut the kids out of the pictures, and glued them "into" the rain forest bulletin board! Kids loved searching for themselves, parents remembered to register, and everyone looked forward to the upcoming adventure!

GET READY FOR THE ADVENTURE OF A LIFETIME!

TREASURE HUNT Bible Adventure

Join us for a week of unforgettable Bible-learning fun at Treasure Hunt Bible Adventure!

Expedition location:
_____
(church name)

The adventure will last:
_____
(VBS dates)

Treasure hunting begins at:
_____
(VBS starting time)

Treasure hunting ends at:
_____
(VBS ending time)

For more clues, call:
_____
(church phone number)

Permission to photocopy this bulletin insert from Group's Treasure Hunt Bible Adventure: Treasure Hunt Bible Adventure Director Manual granted for local church use. Copyright © Group Publishing, Inc., P.O. Box 481, Loveland, CO 80539.

GET READY FOR THE ADVENTURE OF A LIFETIME!

TREASURE HUNT Bible Adventure

Join us for a week of unforgettable Bible-learning fun at Treasure Hunt Bible Adventure!

Expedition location:
_____
(church name)

The adventure will last:
_____
(VBS dates)

Treasure hunting begins at:
_____
(VBS starting time)

Treasure hunting ends at:
_____
(VBS ending time)

For more clues, call:
_____
(church phone number)

Permission to photocopy this bulletin insert from Group's Treasure Hunt Bible Adventure: Treasure Hunt Bible Adventure Director Manual granted for local church use. Copyright © Group Publishing, Inc., P.O. Box 481, Loveland, CO 80539.

PUBLICITY

Your expedition will include these DISCOVERY SITES:

GET READY TO
Discover Amazing Bible Adventures at

TREASURE HUNT
Bible Adventure

DEAR PARENTS:

Get ready for the adventure of a lifetime! This summer, _____ is taking kids on a
(name of church)
rain forest expedition with **TREASURE HUNT BIBLE ADVENTURE.**

Each day your children will dig into Bible learning they can see...hear...touch...and even taste! Unique craft items, team-building games, lively Bible songs, and healthy treats are just a few of the Treasure Hunt Bible Adventure activities that show kids that the Bible is the map and Jesus is the treasure. Children will also enjoy hands-on Bible adventures and daily video visits from Chadder Chipmunk™! Your kids will even participate in a hands-on missions project called Operation Kid-to-Kid.

TREASURE HUNT BIBLE ADVENTURE is great fun for children of all ages; even teenagers will enjoy signing on as "Clue Crew Leaders" who help younger children. And parents, grandparents, and friends are invited to join us each day at _____ for
(time you've scheduled your Treasure Time Finale)
Treasure Time Finale—a daily celebration of God's love you won't want to miss.

So mark _____ on your calendar. The expedi-
(dates of your VBS)
tion starts at _____, and will wrap up at _____. Call
(VBS starting time)   (VBS ending time)
_____ to register your children for a Bible-learning adventure
(church phone number)
they'll never forget.

Sincerely,

Your Treasure Hunt Bible Adventure Director

Permission to photocopy this letter from Group's Treasure Hunt Bible Adventure: Treasure Hunt Bible Adventure Director Manual granted for local church use. Copyright © Group Publishing, Inc., P.O. Box 481, Loveland, CO 80539.

NEWS RELEASE

Adapt the information in this news release to fit your church's Treasure Hunt Bible Adventure program. Then submit typed, double-spaced copies to your local newspapers, radio stations, and TV stations. You may want to check with them for any other specific requirements regarding news releases.

[Name of Church] Invites Children to Dig into the Bible at Treasure Hunt Bible Adventure.

"This year our church is searching for the greatest treasure ever," says [your church pastor's name]. "We're setting off for Treasure Hunt Bible Adventure, where kids won't find any boring reminders of tedious schoolwork. Our Treasure Hunt Bible Adventure program will provide fun, memorable Bible-learning activities for kids of all ages. Each day, kids will sing catchy songs, play teamwork-building games, nibble tasty treats from Treasure Treats, dig into Bible adventures, and create Craft Cave creations they'll take home and play with all summer long. One day, kids will join the Disciple Peter, walking on water. Another day, they'll be thrown on a prison ship with the Apostle Paul!

"Treasure Hunt Bible Adventure is an exploration of God's Word. Kids will get to take part in a hands-on mission project that will reach Spanish-speaking children across the globe. We'll conclude each day with a festive Treasure Time Finale program that gets everyone involved in celebrating what they've learned. Family members and friends are encouraged to join us daily for this special time at [time of Treasure Time Finale]. We hope Treasure Hunt Bible Adventure will help our community discover the treasure of Jesus."

Treasure Hunt Bible Adventure begins at [VBS starting date] and continues through [VBS ending date]. Explorers will meet at [name of church and church address] each day from [VBS starting time] until [VBS ending time]. For information, call [church phone number].

GET READY FOR THE ADVENTURE OF A LIFETIME!

Join us as we explore Treasure Hunt Bible Adventure! You'll enjoy cool crafts and wild games, experience thrilling Bible stories—from a shipwreck to walking on water—sample tasty snacks, and hear lively music. Plus, you'll meet lots of new friends!

EXPEDITION LOCATION:

_____
(church name)

THE ADVENTURE WILL LAST:

_____
(VBS dates)

TREASURE HUNTING BEGINS AT:

_____
(VBS starting time)

TREASURE HUNTING ENDS AT:

_____
(VBS ending time)

FOR MORE CLUES, CALL:

_____
(church phone number)

Permission to photocopy this flier from Group's Treasure Hunt Bible Adventure: Treasure Hunt Bible Adventure Director Manual granted for local church use. Copyright © Group Publishing, Inc., P.O. Box 481, Loveland, CO 80539.

PUBLICITY SKIT

Setting:
Your church. (That should be easy!)

Props:
Kids should be wearing explorers' clothes and the Clue Crew Leader should have a Clue Crew cap and a daily schedule. Mississippi Jones should be dressed in a leather jacket, an old fedora, and tan pants. He'll need a publicity flier or bulletin, and a rope or some other prop that looks like a whip.

Have a few volunteers perform this skit before a worship service, during your announcements, at a midweek program, or during children's church or Sunday school.

Mississippi Jones and the Clue Crew Crusade

(A Clue Crew walks across the stage. Kids are carrying a variety of VBS crafts, such as the Surprise Treasure Chest or Rain Forest Creatures. One child is carrying the crew treasure bag.)

Clue Crew Leader: *(Looking at schedule)* OK, Clue Crew. According to today's schedule, our next Discovery Site is Treasure Treats. Let's go!

Mississippi Jones: *(Bursting onto the scene)* Wait! I'll save you!

Leader: *(Stands in front of kids)* Save us? What do you—who are you?

Jones: I'm the famous explorer and archaeologist, Mississippi Jones. *(Holds up publicity flier or bulletin.)* I received this clue that there might be treasure in this rain forest. But when I got here, I heard some strange native music. I figured that you'd been captured, so I've come to save you!

Leader: We don't need to be saved from anything in this rain forest! What you heard was all the kids at Treasure Hunt Sing & Play! This is Treasure Hunt Bible Adventure. *(Motioning to schedule)* In fact, our daily schedule says that...

Jones: *(Interrupting)* You found a map! Here, I'm an expert in fifteen languages and dialects. Let me read it for you. *(Takes the schedule from leader and begins to read it)* Hmm, looks like modern English to me...something about the Bible showing us the way to trust.

Kids: *(Shout)* Eureka!

Jones: *(Startles and reaches for his "whip")* What's that! Was it a thief after our treasure? Or a snake? I hate snakes!

Leader: No, it's just the kids. When you say the daily Bible Point, they'll shout "Eureka!" That means "I found it!"

Jones: Well, what did they find?

Leader: They're finding lots of great treasures here at Treasure Hunt Bible Adventure. In fact, we just left Bible Exploration, where we experienced a terrible storm!

Jones: Ahh! Sunken treasure! Now we're getting somewhere!

Leader: *(Shakes head)* Not quite. We also went to Chadder's Treasure Hunt Theater. There, the kids used their Bibles as a treasure map to find the riches of God's Word. Now we're headed to Treasure Treats for some "vine" dining at a rain forest picnic.

Jones: *(Suspiciously)* You'd better be sure the food's not poisoned. I remember when I was searching for the lost treasure of the…

Leader: The food won't be poisoned! The preschoolers made it today.

Kids: Let's go! We're getting hungry! I don't want to miss anything!

Jones: Neither do I! This Treasure Hunt Bible Adventure sounds a lot better than the afternoon I had planned. Mind if I join you for Treasure Treats?

Leader: I suppose not. But then we'll have to head to Craft Cave and I'm not sure…

Jones: *(Walking offstage, leading kids)* Oh cool! A cave! I should tell you about the time I was in a cave in the jungles of Egypt…no, wait. Egypt doesn't have jungles. It must have been Australia—yeah, that's it, Australia!

REGISTRATION

Welcoming YOUR EXPLORERS

Making an UNFORGETTABLE IMPRESSION

Treasure Hunt Bible Adventure is a fun place for kids to discover the riches of God's Word. Once kids sample the activities at each Discovery Site, they'll want to explore with you all week long. But you can start generating excitement and enthusiasm for Treasure Hunt Bible Adventure before kids even set foot in a Discovery Site.

The excitement starts with preregistration. About a month before your scheduled Treasure Hunt Bible Adventure program, begin preregistering children in your church. Preregistration is simple: Just make copies of the "Treasure Hunt Bible Adventure Registration Form" (p. 150), and have parents fill them out. Or slip Treasure Hunt Bible Adventure registration cards into your church bulletins. (These registration cards are available from Group Publishing and your local Christian bookstore.) Save the completed registration forms; you'll use them to assign Clue Crews (described on page 137).

To pique kids' (and parents') interest in preregistration, try incorporating some of the following activities:

● **Show the *Discover!* promotional video clip in your church worship service.** This video clip gives everyone in your church a chance to preview Treasure Hunt Bible Adventure. It includes glimpses of each Treasure Hunt Bible Adventure Discovery Site so church members can get "clued in" to all the fun Bible learning that's packed into the Treasure Hunt Bible Adventure program.

● **Have kids in your children's ministry programs design their own Treasure Hunt Bible Adventure posters.** Check out books about the rain forest, treasure hunts, or exploring from your local public library. Talk to kids about treasure hunt things that interest them, such as treasure chests, tropical rain forests, old treasure maps, and clues. Let kids create their own treasure maps, complete with clever clues that lead to valuable treasures! Or, kids can design colorful pictures of a dense, tropical rain forest, filled with monkeys, bugs, birds, and flowers.

● **Have Sunday school classes work together to turn their rooms into rain forests.** Provide butcher paper, markers, green crepe paper streamers, artificial plants, colorful cloth, carpet-roll cores, appliance boxes, and bright feathers. Encourage kids to hang crepe paper "vines" from ceilings and windows, or to create jungle huts from appliance boxes. Kids may want to bring in their own stuffed animals to add to the decor. Kids who are attending Treasure Hunt Bible Adventure can sign their names or attach their photos on the finished trees

Field Test Findings

Several weeks before our Treasure Hunt Bible Adventure began, the children's church director had kids make rain forest pictures and decorations to get everyone thinking about VBS. Not only did kids get excited about the theme, but our decorations committee got a huge boost!

A CLUE FOR YOU!

Many churches use preregistration time as a simple fund-raising time. Ask adults to "sponsor" one or more children who will attend VBS. (Post the total number of children you're expecting at VBS so people have an idea of the number of kids you need to sponsor.) The sponsorship fee can be monetary, or it may be a food donation for Treasure Treats. Each time someone sponsors a child, tape a large paper leaf or tropical flower to the wall near your registration area. We've heard of churches funding their entire VBS program through these easy donations!

and vines. Discovery Site Leaders or other adults might also enjoy this project!

● **Chart your preregistration with the Treasure Hunt Bible Adventure theme poster.** If you ordered the Treasure Hunt Bible Adventure theme poster, hang it in a conspicuous location. Each time someone preregisters, place a paper leaf or colorful flower around the poster. When it's time for Treasure Hunt Bible Adventure to begin, you'll have a wonderful wall decoration and a church filled with eager explorers!

EXTRA IDEA!

If you want to start your rain forest trek with extra style and pizazz, consider planning an all-church treasure hunt adventure. Decorate your fellowship hall, church lawn, or a nearby park, and set up one or more of the following "discovery sites."

● Use face paints to create monkey, tiger, or butterfly designs on kids' faces.
● Hide foil-covered chocolate coins in a roped-off area and allow participants to search for edible treasures.
● Set up one of the "Jungle Gym Gem" activities from pages 13-18 of the Jungle Gym Games Leader Manual. Kids and adults both will love the Backward Waterfall, as well as an Archaeological Dig.
● Set out an inflatable pool filled with water. Drop in plastic coins, gems, or other "treasures" and allow participants to search for sunken treasures...with their toes!
● Provide several audiocassette recorders, loaded with blank tapes. Have kids and adults make their best jungle noises.
● Set up an obstacle course (just like Indiana Jones might go through) that participants must go in, under, around, and through to reach a treasure.
● Provide tropical fruits, such as mangoes, pineapples, and guava for everyone to sample. You'll also want to set out a treasure chest filled with "valuable" treats such as Hershey's Nuggets chocolates, foil-covered chocolate coins, 100 Grand candy bars, or candy necklaces and rings.
● Set out newspapers and markers and have kids create their own treasure maps.

The excitement continues as kids arrive at Treasure Hunt Bible Adventure. At registration, remember that some families from your community are coming into contact with your church for the first time. You don't want their first impression to be of long, boring registration lines. To make an unforgettable impression, try the following ideas:

● **Prepare a large "Welcome, Explorers!" sign, and post it behind your registration table.** Ask an artistic person in your church to write "Welcome, Explorers! Your Adventure Begins Here" in large block letters on a large sheet of poster board or butcher paper. Decorate the sign with paints, markers, old maps, or fake jewels for a festive look.

● **Set up the Treasure Hunt Bible Adventure Starter Kit can as a display on your registration table.** Set the can on top of a jungle-print tablecloth (or sheet of wrapping paper) for a rain forest feel. You may want to fill the can with Hershey's Nuggets chocolates and miniature 100 Grand candy bars for kids to enjoy as they register.

● **Play the *Treasure Hunt Sing & Play* audiocassette or CD.** The fun,

upbeat music will provide a fun, festive atmosphere.

● **Use a Chadder Chipmunk puppet (available from Group Publishing and your local Christian bookstore) to greet kids who are waiting in the registration line.** Younger children who might be afraid to leave their parents or caregivers will be reassured by this fuzzy friend—especially when they hear that they'll get to see him each day in the *Chadder's Treasure Hunt Adventure* video. And if you've used Group's VBS in the past, children will delight in seeing Chadder—their familiar, furry friend!

● **Pass out sample Treasure Treats.** You can use a snack from the Treasure Treats Leader Manual or you can come up with your own. Be sure to include drinks—especially if the weather's hot.

Gear up for an unforgettable treasure hunt!

Setting Up CLUE CREWS

One week before Treasure Hunt Bible Adventure begins, assign preregistered kids to Clue Crews. Participating in Clue Crews is an important part of kids' Treasure Hunt Bible Adventure experience, so use care and consideration when making Clue Crew assignments. Follow the guidelines given in the planning section of this manual under "One Week Before Treasure Hunt Bible Adventure" (p. 49). If you don't know very many of the kids who will attend Treasure Hunt Bible Adventure, ask Sunday school teachers or other Christian education workers to help you assign kids to crews.

Step One: Inventory Your Registrations

● When you're ready to assign crews, make nine copies of the "Age-Level Roster" form (p. 147). Label the forms with grades K, 1, 2, 3, 4, and 5; do the same using "3-year-olds," "4-year-olds," and "5-year-olds" (for 5-year-olds who have not yet attended kindergarten). List the names of preregistered kids on the appropriate age-level rosters.

● Count how many kids have preregistered for your Treasure Hunt Bible Adventure, and divide them into two groups: elementary-age children and preschool-age children. Elementary-age children have completed kindergarten, fifth grade, or any grade in between. Be sure to check forms carefully; some families may have registered more than one child on one form. If children who have completed sixth grade want to participate in your program, that's OK; keep in mind, though, that most of the Treasure Hunt Bible Adventure activities are designed for

A CLUE FOR YOU!

If you have a willing seamstress or tailor in your congregation, have him or her sew the life-size Chadder Chipmunk costume (pattern available from Group Publishing and your local Christian bookstore). Then ask a volunteer to play Chadder and greet children at registration. Chadder's antics and warmth will be the perfect start to Treasure Hunt Bible Adventure!

A CLUE FOR YOU!

Prayerfully consider the responsibility of setting up Clue Crews. These small groups have a powerful impact on children, helping them form special relationships and memories.

Field Test Findings

When we used sixth-graders as assistant crew leaders, we learned that, depending on interests and maturity level, some were interested in doing the crafts, games, and snacks as participants rather than being crew leaders. Use your best judgment as each situation arises. Be flexible so you can provide the best possible experience for your "tweenagers."

Once you've determined the number of Clue Crews you'll have, ask volunteers to help create a complete Clue Crew treasure bag for each Clue Crew. Place a permanent marker, five name badges, five one-yard lengths of Mini Jungle Vine, five Elementary or Preschool Student Books, and five elementary or preschool Treasure Hunt sticker sheets inside each Clue Crew treasure bag. (You'll also need five Bible highlighters in each elementary treasure bag.) On Day 1, simply give each Clue Crew Leader a treasure bag.

slightly younger kids. Treasure Hunt Bible Adventure is designed to use young people in grades six and higher in leadership roles; encourage mature sixth-graders to serve as Assistant Clue Crew Leaders. For other ideas about how upper-elementary kids can participate in Treasure Hunt Bible Adventure, see page 28.

Step Two: Determine How Many Clue Crews You'll Have

● Each Clue Crew will have no more than five kids and one adult or teenage Clue Crew Leader. (Preschool crews may have a high school leader.) Divide the total number of preregistered elementary-age kids by five to discover how many elementary Clue Crews you'll have. Do the same with preschool preregistrations. Use the line below to help you determine this.

If you want to encourage kids to bring their friends to Treasure Hunt Bible Adventure, you may want to place only three or four kids in each crew. This will allow you to add to your crews.

Once you've determined the number of preschool and elementary crews you'll need, check to see that you've recruited enough Clue Crew Leaders. Remember that you'll need a Clue Crew Leader for every crew, plus a few extra leaders on hand on Day 1.

Number of (elementary or preschool) kids _____/ at five kids per crew = Number of **Clue Crews**_____.

Step Three: Assign Clue Crews

● Photocopy the "Clue Crew Roster" form (p. 148). You'll need one form for every four Clue Crews.

● Assign a Clue Crew Leader to each Clue Crew. It's helpful to indicate whether the leader is an adult (A), a teenager (T), or junior higher (J).

● **Preschool Clue Crews**

Gather the age-level rosters for ages three, four, and five. Beginning with the three-year-old age-level roster, assign one child from each preschool age-level roster to each preschool Clue Crew. Since each crew has five spaces, you'll have more than one representative of some age levels in each crew. Remember, it's helpful to have a mixture of preschool ages in each crew so crew leaders can work with three-year-olds, while five-year-olds may be a bit more self-sufficient. Be sure to check off the names on the age-level rosters as you assign them to crews.

● **Elementary Clue Crews**

Gather the elementary age-level rosters. Beginning with the kindergarten age-level roster, assign one child from each age-level roster to each Clue Crew. Since each crew has only five spaces, you won't be able to have every age level in every crew. Check off the names on the age-level rosters as you assign them to crews. Refer to the examples on page 139 for ways to spread age levels evenly among your Clue Crews.

You aren't *required* to group children in combined-age Clue Crews, but we strongly recommend it because it works so well. Children, young and old alike, help one another throughout their time together. Plus you'll minimize discipline problems because the diversity frees children from the need to compete with peers of the same age. For more information on the benefits of combining ages, see page 25.

If you have an equal number of children in each grade level,
- fill one-third of your crews with kids who have completed kindergarten and grades two through five.
- fill one-third of your crews with kids who have completed grades one through five.
- fill one-third of your crews with kids who have completed kindergarten through grade four.

If you have an abundance of younger children,
- group kindergartners, second-graders, third-graders, and fifth-graders together. Assign two kindergartners to each crew if necessary. Remind Clue Crew Leaders to encourage the fifth-graders to help younger children. Fifth-graders might even be named "Assistant Clue Crew Leaders."
- group kids in grades one through four together. Assign two first-graders to each crew if necessary.

If you have an abundance of older children,
- group kindergartners, first-graders, second-graders, and fourth-graders together. Assign two fourth-graders to each crew if necessary.
- group grades two through five together. Assign two fifth-graders to each crew if necessary.

If you have fewer than five kids per Clue Crew,
- vary the age-level mix, if possible, so you'll have open spaces in your program at every age level. These spaces can be filled by kids who haven't preregistered.

Step Four: Complete the Master List
- Double-check to make sure you've assigned each participant to a Clue Crew. Then write kids' Clue Crew numbers on their registration forms next to their names.
- Alphabetize the registration forms, and then transfer kids' names and crew numbers to the "Alphabetical Master List" (p. 149). Put a "P" in the crew-number space next to each preschooler's name.
- Give the preschool registration forms, age-level rosters, and Clue Crew rosters to the Preschool Bible Treasure Land Director.

Bring the "Age-Level Roster" lists, "Clue Crew Roster" lists, and "Alphabetical Master List" with you to registration!

Field Test Findings

We had Clue Crew Leaders make their crew posters during the training session (see pp. 101-118). Not only did this save time on the first day of VBS, but it got the crew leaders thinking (and praying) about their crews before VBS had even started. Besides, they did an amazing job and made the posters bright and colorful!

Field Test Findings

We posted the crew posters numerically, so kids could easily find their crew leaders on the first day. Later in the week, crew leaders mentioned that kids sitting in the back rows were feeling a little disconnected from what was happening up front. So, midweek, we rotated the crew posters so new kids could sit near the front and really tune in to the program. It was a super way to keep everyone "clued in" to the action!

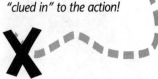

Let Clue Crew Leaders HELP WITH TREASURE HUNT SIGN-IN

Clue Crew Leaders can help you breeze through registration! They meet and greet kids and help keep kids busy while others are standing in line. Read on to find out how Clue Crew Leaders help make registration a snap.

Clue Crew Leader Registration Supplies

Each Clue Crew Leader will need the following supplies:
- a permanent marker,
- colorful washable markers or posters,
- one sheet of poster board,
- one Clue Crew treasure bag,
- a copy of the "Clue Crew Roster" for his or her crew, and
- masking tape.

Each child will need a Student Book, a Treasure Hunt sticker sheet, and a name badge strung on one yard of Mini Jungle Vine. Give these items to the Clue Crew Leaders and have them store the items in their Clue Crew treasure bags.

Clue Crew Leader Registration Procedures

- Give each Clue Crew Leader a Treasure Hunt Bible Adventure cap to wear. This helps Discovery Site Leaders and kids recognize crew leaders.
- When Clue Crew Leaders arrive, they'll write their Clue Crew numbers on sheets of poster board then hang the number posters *where they can be seen easily* in the Treasure Hunt Sing & Play area. It helps if leaders hang the posters in numerical order.
- After children complete the registration process, they'll meet their Clue Crew Leaders by their crew-number posters in Treasure Hunt Sing & Play.
- Clue Crew Leaders will greet kids and welcome them to Treasure Hunt Bible Adventure. Leaders will use permanent markers to write kids' names and crew numbers on their name badges. If additional kids have been assigned to Clue Crews during registration, Clue Crew Leaders will update their copies of the "Clue Crew Roster."
- Clue Crews will work on decorating their crew-number posters while they wait for others to arrive. This is a fun time for Clue Crew Leaders and crew members to get acquainted.

Registration Day IS HERE

Registration Supplies

For registration, you'll need the following supplies:
- entry decorations such as real or artificial trees, stuffed animals, a treasure chest, and a rolled-up treasure map
- three tables
- four signs:
  ✔ "Preregistered—kindergarten through fifth grade"
  ✔ "Walk-in registration—kindergarten through fifth grade"
  ✔ two "Preschool registration" signs with arrows pointing to the Preschool Bible Treasure Land
- two copies of each completed elementary "Clue Crew Roster" (p. 148)
- one copy of each completed preschool "Clue Crew Roster" (p. 148)
- three copies of each completed elementary "Age-Level Roster" (p. 147)
- two copies of each completed preschool "Age-Level Roster" (p. 147)
- two copies of the completed "Alphabetical Master List" (p. 149)
- plenty of pens and pencils
- at least five volunteers, including the Registrar
- chairs for your volunteers
- blank copies of the "Treasure Hunt Bible Adventure Registration Form" (p. 150)

Registration Setup

Before registration, set up two tables in your church's foyer or entry area. If weather permits, you may want to set up your tables outside to allow more room. (It's a good idea to place these tables far apart to avoid a bottleneck.) Put the "Preregistered—kindergarten through fifth grade" sign above one table. Put the "Walk-in registration—kindergarten through fifth grade" sign above the other table. Set up chairs for your volunteers at each table. Be sure to place your signs high enough for everyone to see clearly!

Preregistered Table

On the table below the preregistered sign, place
- a copy of the completed "Alphabetical Master List" (p. 149),
- a copy of each completed "Clue Crew Roster" (p. 148), and
- several pencils.

A CLUE FOR YOU!

Having Clue Crew Leaders write kids' names on their name badges is a nice way for leaders to learn the names of their crew members. Plus, they can make them all large and legible!

A CLUE FOR YOU!

You may want to give each Clue Crew Leader a few extra name badges and one-yard lengths of Mini Jungle Vine for walk-in registrants who may join their crews.

Field Test Findings

We discovered that it was helpful to tape lists and rosters to the registration tables. That way they didn't blow away or get lost or torn. Plus registration helpers had easy access to all information and could easily scan the lists to find a child's name.

Walk-In Registration Table

On the table below the walk-in registration sign, place
- a copy of each completed elementary "Age-Level Roster" (p. 147),
- a copy of each completed "Clue Crew Roster" (p. 148),
- copies of the "Registration Form" (p. 150), and
- several pens or pencils.

> ### Take the Express Lane!
> Consider an "Express Preregistered Check-In" system. Have a couple of volunteers stand at the entryway, holding copies of the "Alphabetical Master List." Kids who are preregistered can tell the "Express Checkers" their names and have the Checkers look at the list to see which Clue Crews kids are in. Or if you're low on volunteers, enlarge your "Alphabetical Master List," and post several copies of it near your registration area. Kids (and parents) can check the list to find what Clue Crews they're on and then simply find their crew numbers and Clue Crew Leaders!

Preschool Registration Table

Set up a table (or several if you have more than twenty-five preschoolers) outside your Preschool Bible Treasure Land area. Put the two "Preschool registration" signs (with arrows pointing to the Preschool Bible Treasure Land) near your main registration area.

On the preschool registration table(s), place
- a copy of each completed preschool "Age-Level Roster" (p. 147),
- a copy of each preschool "Clue Crew Roster" (p. 148),
- blank copies of the "Registration Form" (p. 150), and
- several pencils.

Registration: HERE THEY COME!

1. Arrange for your registration workers (including Clue Crew Leaders) to arrive at least thirty minutes *before* registration is scheduled to begin.

2. Cut apart the individual "Clue Crew Roster" lists from the third set of "Clue Crew Roster" lists you copied. As Clue Crew Leaders arrive, give each a copy of his or her crew roster.

3. Send elementary Clue Crew Leaders to the Treasure Hunt Sing & Play area and preschool Clue Crew Leaders to Preschool Bible Treasure Land. Explain that as kids arrive, they'll find their Clue Crew numbers at the registration tables and then join their crew leaders and other Clue Crew members in Treasure Hunt Sing & Play or Preschool Bible Treasure Land.

4. Assign two workers to the preregistration table, two workers to the walk-in table, and at least one worker to the preschool table.

5. Go over the registration instructions for each area (preregistered, walk-in registration, and preschool). Answer any questions workers have, and offer the following helpful hints:

● Kindly insist that each participant fill out a complete registration form, including all pertinent health and emergency information. *This is very important!*

● If families have both preschool and elementary children, encourage them to go to the preschool area first. This will keep preschoolers from getting fidgety as they wait for their parents to register their older siblings.

● Walk-in registration will naturally take more time. As families are filling out their registration forms, scan the Clue Crew rosters for openings. This will help you complete Clue Crew assignments quickly.

After you've answered all the questions, have registration workers and Clue Crew Leaders take their places. You're ready to welcome kids to Treasure Hunt Bible Adventure!

It's important that you have a completed registration form for *each child,* not just one for each family! When families place all their children on one form, it can be difficult to find information that's specific to each child.

> **Important!**
> It's important that you know at all times who is in each Clue Crew. In an emergency or if a parent needs to pick up a child midprogram, you'll want an accurate "map" of where everyone is.

After REGISTRATION

Field Test Findings

It really is important to touch base with Clue Crew Leaders after the first day (or even after each day!). We made a few "tweaks" in Clue Crews, such as pairing up a less-experienced crew leader with a veteran leader. By catching problems or miscommunications early on, everyone enjoyed a smoother program!

Field Test Findings

Through our field tests and from customer feedback, we've learned (oftentimes, the hard way) that two-year olds really are too young for a program like this. Kindly insist that only three-year olds may join the expedition—everyone (especially those little ones) will appreciate your efforts in the long run!

After registration on Day 1, shout out a loud, "Eureka!" Your biggest job is done! Read on to find out how you can ensure that Days 2 through 5 are successful.

● **Leave your registration tables in place.** You'll want to continue welcoming children as they arrive on Days 2 through 5, as well as registering any newcomers. Tape the "Alphabetical Master List" to the table, and set out several pencils or pens. To chart attendance, let children (or parents) check each day's box as they come to Treasure Hunt Bible Adventure.

● **Check in with Discovery Site Leaders and Clue Crew Leaders.** Even if you've mapped everything out ahead of time, unforeseen glitches can mar your treasure hunt! After you've gone through one day's activities, meet with your treasure hunt staff to evaluate how things went. Discovery Site Leaders may find that they need additional supplies or alternative room assignments. Inexperienced Clue Crew Leaders may be having trouble handling unruly children in their Clue Crews. If this is the case, you may need to reassign some children to different crews or rearrange your groups so that Clue Crews with inexperienced leaders visit Discovery Sites with crews that have experienced leaders.

● **Update your "Alphabetical Master List" and "Clue Crew Rosters" as needed.** Be sure to check with the volunteers at the walk-in table. Kids who completed walk-in registration on Day 1 can be added to the "Alphabetical Master List" for speedier check-in through the rest of the week. If you've rearranged your Clue Crews, make sure each Clue Crew receives an updated "Clue Crew Roster."

You did it! Now sit back and enjoy the adventure!

TREASURE HUNT BIBLE ADVENTURE
Registration Instructions

Photocopy these instructions, and place copies in all registration areas. Have registration workers highlight their areas of responsibility.

Preschool: Preregistered and Walk-In

Preschool registration will take place _____.

1. Greet family members or caregivers with a warm smile. Thank them for bringing the children to Treasure Hunt Bible Adventure.
2. Ask for each child's name and age (three, four, or five years old). Greet each child by name, and thank him or her for coming.

If a child has completed kindergarten or is older than six, send the family to the elementary preregistered line.

3. Have parents or caregivers complete registration forms for unregistered children.
4. Locate each registered child's name on the "Alphabetical Master List," and place a check mark on the Day 1 box to indicate that he or she is present.
5. If a child is a walk-in, scan the preschool "Clue Crew Roster" lists to find an appropriate Clue Crew to place him or her in. Add the child's name to the "Clue Crew Roster" list as well as to the "Alphabetical Master List."
6. Point out the child's Clue Crew Leader, and have a Preschool Bible Treasure Land volunteer guide the child to the Clue Crew Leader.
7. Tell the family members or caregivers that they can pick up their preschoolers in the Treasure Time Finale area each day. Assure them that an adult or teenage Clue Crew Leader will stay with children until the family members or caregivers arrive.

Elementary: Preregistered

Elementary registration will take place _____.

1. Greet family members or caregivers with a warm smile. Thank them for bringing the children to Treasure Hunt Bible Adventure.
2. Ask for each child's name and the grade he or she last completed (kindergarten through fifth grade). Greet each child by name, and thank him or her for coming.

If a child has not yet attended kindergarten, send the family to Preschool Bible Treasure Land for registration.

3. Locate each child's name on the "Alphabetical Master List" or, if a child's name isn't on the list, send the family to the walk-in table to complete a new registration form.
4. Put a check mark by each child's name to indicate that he or she is present at Treasure Hunt Bible Adventure. Then tell the child his or her Clue Crew number and crew leader's name.
5. Direct children to the Treasure Hunt Sing & Play area, and explain that crew leaders are waiting there with name badges. Tell children to look for the large signs with their crew numbers on them.
6. Tell the family members or caregivers what time they can pick up their children each day. Encourage them to come early and participate in Treasure Time Finale.

Permission to photocopy this handout from Group's Treasure Hunt Bible Adventure: Treasure Hunt Bible Adventure Director Manual granted for local church use. Copyright © Group Publishing, Inc., P.O. Box 481, Loveland, CO 80539.

TREASURE HUNT BIBLE ADVENTURE
Registration Instructions

Elementary: Walk-In Registration
Elementary registration will take place _____.

1. Greet family members or caregivers with a warm smile. Thank them for bringing the children to Treasure Hunt Bible Adventure.
2. Ask for each child's name and the grade he or she last completed (kindergarten through fifth grade). Greet each child by name, and thank him or her for coming.

If a child has not yet attended kindergarten, send the family to Preschool Bible Treasure Land for registration.

3. Add each child's name to the appropriate "Age-Level Roster." Have the child's parent or caregiver complete a registration form.
4. While parents fill out registration forms, assign each child to a Clue Crew. Refer to the "Clue Crew Rosters" to see which crews have openings. Look for a Clue Crew *without* a member in that child's grade. *If you have questions about assigning children to Clue Crews, see your Treasure Hunt Director!*
5. Write each child's Clue Crew number on his or her completed registration form. (Later you'll need to add the new name and Clue Crew assignment to the "Alphabetical Master List.")
6. Direct children to the Treasure Hunt Sing & Play area, and explain that crew leaders are waiting there with name badges. Tell children to look for the large signs with their crew numbers on them.
7. Tell the family members or caregivers what time they can pick up their children each day. Encourage them to come early and participate in Treasure Time Finale.

AGE-LEVEL ROSTER

Grade: _____

CLUE CREW ROSTER

Clue Crew Number: _____

Clue Crew Leader: _____

Clue Crew Members

1. _____
2. _____
3. _____
4. _____
5. _____

Clue Crew Number: _____

Clue Crew Leader: _____

Clue Crew Members

1. _____
2. _____
3. _____
4. _____
5. _____

Clue Crew Number: _____

Clue Crew Leader: _____

Clue Crew Members

1. _____
2. _____
3. _____
4. _____
5. _____

Clue Crew Number: _____

Clue Crew Leader: _____

Clue Crew Members

1. _____
2. _____
3. _____
4. _____
5. _____

Permission to photocopy this handout from Group's Treasure Hunt Bible Adventure: Treasure Hunt Bible Adventure Director Manual granted for local church use. Copyright © Group Publishing, Inc., P.O. Box 481, Loveland, CO 80539.

ALPHABETICAL MASTER LIST

Name	Clue Crew Number	Day 1	Day 2	Day 3	Day 4	Day 5
____	____	☐	☐	☐	☐	☐
____	____	☐	☐	☐	☐	☐
____	____	☐	☐	☐	☐	☐
____	____	☐	☐	☐	☐	☐
____	____	☐	☐	☐	☐	☐
____	____	☐	☐	☐	☐	☐
____	____	☐	☐	☐	☐	☐
____	____	☐	☐	☐	☐	☐
____	____	☐	☐	☐	☐	☐
____	____	☐	☐	☐	☐	☐
____	____	☐	☐	☐	☐	☐
____	____	☐	☐	☐	☐	☐
____	____	☐	☐	☐	☐	☐
____	____	☐	☐	☐	☐	☐
____	____	☐	☐	☐	☐	☐
____	____	☐	☐	☐	☐	☐
____	____	☐	☐	☐	☐	☐
____	____	☐	☐	☐	☐	☐
____	____	☐	☐	☐	☐	☐
____	____	☐	☐	☐	☐	☐
____	____	☐	☐	☐	☐	☐

Permission to photocopy this handout from Group's Treasure Hunt Bible Adventure: Treasure Hunt Bible Adventure Director Manual granted for local church use. Copyright © Group Publishing, Inc., P.O. Box 481, Loveland, CO 80539.

TREASURE HUNT BIBLE ADVENTURE
Registration Form
(one per child)

Name: _____

Street address: _____

City: _____ State: _____ ZIP: _____

Home Telephone: (_____) _____ Age: _____

Last school grade completed: _____

In case of emergency, contact: _____

Mother: _____

Father: _____

Other: _____

Allergies or other medical conditions: _____

Home church: _____

Clue Crew number (for church use only): _____

Daily Staff DEVOTIONS

Plan to meet with your Discovery Site Leaders and Clue Crew Leaders for fifteen to twenty minutes before your program begins each day. Use this time to give announcements, address questions or concerns, and pray together. Ministering to children is rewarding but hard work, so you may also want to refresh your staff daily with an encouraging devotional. The devotions below tie into the Treasure Hunt Bible Adventure daily Bible Points.

Day 1

Safe in the Storm

Preparation
You'll need a Bible and an umbrella.

Devotion
Gather everyone in a circle, then say: **This week at Treasure Hunt Bible Adventure, we'll help children discover the greatest treasure of all—Jesus! The Bible story we'll focus on today is about someone who realized that Jesus truly was a treasure. Turn to a partner and talk about ways that Jesus is a treasure to you.** Allow a few moments for partners to share, and then ask:

● **How is Jesus a treasure to you?** Allow a few volunteers to share their responses.

Say: **In today's Bible story, Peter and the other disciples are caught in a frightening storm. Although the weather today may not be frightening, we may experience a few "storms" along the way. God's Word gives us clear direction for "stormy" times in life.** Read aloud John 14:1. Ask:

● **When is it hardest for you to trust God?**
● **What helps you put your faith in God?**

Open your umbrella, and say: **An umbrella can be quite a comfort during a storm! Just as Peter discovered safety and reassurance in Jesus, we can rely on Jesus to shelter and protect us through the difficulties we face.**

I'll pass this umbrella around the circle. When it comes to you, say "I can trust God when..." then tell a time when it's hard for you to trust God. You might say, "I can trust God when your Clue Crew is a

A CLUE FOR YOU!
Due to last-minute details, it can be tough to set aside time to meet *before* VBS. You may want to use these devotions after each day's program, as a reflection and encouragement to your staff.

153

little wild," or "I can trust God when things are hard at home."

Begin by saying, "I can trust God..." and then finish the sentence by telling about a time you need to trust God. Pass the umbrella to the person on your right. When the umbrella comes back to you, close it and set it aside.

Say: **When we trust in Jesus, we come to understand what a true treasure he is.** Pray: **Dear God, thank you for the opportunity to share your treasure with the children here. Help us to show kids that they can put their trust in you, even when life seems "stormy" or out of control. Thank you for being our shelter all the time. In Jesus' name, amen.**

Day 2

Love Languages

Preparation

You'll need a Bible, the *Treasure Hunt Sing & Play* audiocassette or CD, an audiocassette or CD player, index cards, and a pencil. Before your staff gathers, write each of the following phrases on an index card:

Say, "Te amo." (This means "I love you" in Spanish.)
Hug someone.
Say, "You brighten my day."
Scratch someone's back.
Say, "I appreciate you."
Pat someone on the back.
Say, "I like talking with you."
Say, "I'm glad you're here."

Write enough cards so each person in your group will have one. It's OK if the messages are repeated.

Devotion

Say: **Today you're going to send special messages to each other. I'm going to give each person a card. Silently read what's written on your card. It may be a spoken message, or an action you'll perform. Then I'll turn on some music—that's your cue to get up and move around the room. Find someone and do or say what's written on your card. Then exchange cards and find new people to interact with. Continue to exchange cards each time you interact with someone. When I turn off the music, gather in a circle and sit down. Ready?**

Turn on the *Treasure Hunt Sing & Play* audiocassette or CD. You may want to play the song "Put a Little Love in Your Heart" or "Jesus Loves Me." When the song ends, turn off the cassette player and wait for everyone to sit down. Ask:

• **What message were you passing along?**
• **How did it feel to send your message?**
• **What was it like to receive the different messages?**

Say: **Today kids will discover how highly Jesus values loving words and actions.** Read aloud John 13:34. Continue: **But Jesus didn't just tell his**

disciples to love—he demonstrated it. Ask:

• **How can you show love to the kids in your crew or Discovery Site today?**
• **How do you think they might respond to your actions and words?**
• **What might stop you from showing love to a child today?**

Say: **Jesus didn't choose an easy way to love the disciples. He could have just washed their hands! But Jesus knelt down and washed their dirty, smelly feet. Some of the kids you contact today may be unpleasant, too. But just as Jesus modeled loving words and actions, we can show children how to love, too.**

Pray: **Dear God, thank you for showing us love in so many ways. Help us model your love to the children we meet today. Help them understand how much you love them and how they can love others in return. Give us creative ways to love those who seem so unlovable. Open our eyes to those who need your love the most. Amen.**

Day 3

It's a Privilege to Pray

Preparation

You'll need a Bible and a bag of candy or other treats.

Devotion

Form two groups. Huddle with the first group and explain that you've brought treats for everyone. It's the job of the first group to tell the others about the treats, without speaking. Then huddle with the members of the second group and explain that they're to put their hands over their ears and sing "Amazing Grace" as loudly as possible. Bring your two groups together, and say "Go!"

After about thirty seconds, call time and have both groups gather together. Distribute the candy and ask:

• **How did you feel during this activity?**
• **What made communication difficult?**
• **How was this experience like or unlike prayer?**

Say: **Today the kids will hear about the importance of prayer. Prayer is simply communication with God—something that's important for Christian growth.** Ask:

• **What keeps us from communicating with God?**
• **What keeps kids from communicating with God?**
• **What "treats" await us when we pray and listen effectively?**

Say: **Prayer is vital to our relationship with God. Jesus modeled prayer beautifully in John 17, when he prayed for his disciples and then for us.** Read aloud John 17:20. Ask:

• **How does it feel to know that Jesus prayed for you?**

Say: **Jesus loved us so much that he brought us before his Father, praying for us before we were even born! Let's turn to God right now**

and thank him for that privilege.

Allow a few moments of silent prayer, before closing with a prayer similar to this one. Pray: **God, thank you for the privilege of prayer. We want to talk with you and build our relationship with you. Help us to keep the lines of communication open, free from distractions and busyness. In Jesus' name, amen.**

Day 4

Good News!

Preparation

You'll need a Bible, construction paper, tape, and markers.

Devotion

Have group members scatter around the room. Say: **Think of some really exciting news you'd like to share today. Maybe your son's soccer team won last night, or you heard that your grandmother is getting out of the hospital. Maybe your good news is that you've made it through three days of VBS! Now, place your hand over your mouth and shout your good news on the count of three. Ready? One, two, three.**

Allow group members to shout their news at once while covering their mouths with their hands. Say: **Hmm. I couldn't really hear that very well. This time, you can keep your hand away from your mouth, but only whisper your good news. Ready? One, two, three.**

Allow everyone to whisper their news at once. Say: **Nope, I still couldn't hear it very well. OK, this time, go ahead and shout it out. Ready? One, two, three.**

Allow everyone to shout their good news at once. Then gather everyone in a circle. Ask:

- **How do you normally share good news?**
- **How was this experience like sharing good news?**
- **When you have good news, who do you tell first?**

Say: **Today, kids will hear the greatest news of all.** Read aloud John 3:16. **Pretend the person sitting next to you is a child at VBS. Tell him or her why this passage is such great news.** Let partners share for a moment; then have them trade roles. Ask:

- **What keeps us from telling children the good news about Jesus?**
- **How can you overcome those barriers?**

Say: **Today, children will have the opportunity to discover that Jesus is the greatest treasure they'll ever have. That's amazing, wonderful, exciting news!** Give each person a sheet of construction paper and a marker. Say: **Write out John 3:16 on your sheet of paper, then roll the paper into a megaphone.** Provide tape so individuals can tape the rolled papers into megaphones.

After a minute or two, say: **Now let's use our megaphones to *really* shout the wonderful news of Jesus. On the count of three, shout the**

A CLUE FOR YOU!

On Day 4, children will hear the message of Jesus' death and resurrection. Since this may be a natural time for children to ask questions about salvation, you may want to photocopy and distribute the "Helping Children Know Jesus" section (p. 171) to each staff member.

words to John 3:16 into your megaphone. Ready? One, two, three!

When everyone has shouted the good news, pray: **Lord Jesus, thank you for loving us enough to die for us. We're so grateful that we can shout and celebrate the wonderful news of your love and forgiveness. We pray for those children who will hear that good news today. Open their hearts so they may come to know you. In Jesus' name, amen.**

Day 5

Walking on Eggshells

Preparation

You'll need a Bible, a plastic sheet or tablecloth, three or four raw eggs, and strips of cloth or bandannas. Before everyone arrives, place the plastic sheet on the floor, and place the eggs randomly across it.

Devotion

Form two groups and have them stand on opposite sides of the sheet. Choose three or four volunteers and blindfold them, using the strips of cloth or bandannas. Gather the blindfolded volunteers at one end of the sheet, then say: **Your goal is to cross the sheet without breaking any eggs. The group on your right will shout good, helpful directions; while the group on your left will try to distract and confuse you. Ready? Go!**

Send the volunteers across the sheet, one at a time. After they've all crossed (whether or not any eggs were broken), allow them to remove their blindfolds. Ask:

● **What was it like to cross the sheet?**

● **What was it like to shout the good, helpful instructions? the distractions?**

● **How is this like trying to make good decisions in life?**

Say: **God has given us a helpful "map" for life. The Bible gives excellent guidance, when other things in life try to distract or confuse us.** Ask:

● **How was this activity similar to obeying God? How is it different?**

● **How do the commands in the Bible help you in life?**

Say: **"Navigating" our way in life can be difficult. Children face just as many—if not more—distractions and frustrations as we do. That's why it's so important that they understand that God has given them clear, understandable instructions in the Bible.**

Pray: **Dear God, thank you for giving us your Word to guide us through life. Help us reach children so they may learn to turn to the Bible as they make their way in life. Guide us today and give us wisdom as we reach children for you, amen.**

Bells and WHISTLES

You have all the basic Treasure Hunt Bible Adventure materials in your Starter Kit. If you want to add sparkle and pizazz to your program, check out some of the following items.

Discovery Site Leader Resources

● **Bamboo whistle**—You and your Discovery Site Leaders will keep kids' attention the easy way with these wooden whistles. Children love the exotic, flute-like sound and will easily hear it in a crowded room or on a playing field. As Treasure Hunt Director, you'll use a bamboo whistle to let Clue Crews know when it's time to "search for" their next Discovery Sites. Encourage Discovery Site Leaders to use the whistles any time they need to get kids' attention.

● **Treasure Hunt Bible Adventure staff T-shirts**—Outfit your Discovery Site Leaders and other helpers in style. These shirts are bright, eye-catching additions to your décor. Kids and adults will love them, and they'll wear them even after Treasure Hunt Bible Adventure is over.

● ***Treasure Hunt Sing & Play* audiocassette or *Treasure Hunt Sing & Play Music & Clip Art* CD**—Reinforce Bible learning by providing each Discovery Site Leader with his or her own *Treasure Hunt Sing & Play* audiocassette or CD. Kids can hum along as they work in Craft Cave, play Jungle Gym Games, and enjoy Treasure Treats. You can also offer this audiocassette or CD to families to reinforce Bible learning at home.

● ***Treasure Hunt Sing & Play* Transparencies**—Project song lyrics onto a large screen to make it even easier for kids (and adults) to follow along.

● **Treasure Treats chef hat**—Tall, starched, and white, this classic paper chef hat helps your Treasure Treats Leader look the part! Order one for your Treasure Treats Leader, or order several so kids can join in the food-preparation fun.

● ***Preschool Bible Treasure Land* audiocassette**—Provide upbeat music for your youngest explorers. This cassette includes the Treasure Hunt Bible Adventure theme song, "I've Found Me a Treasure," as well as other special songs and stories just for preschoolers.

Additional Treasure Hunt Resources

- **Treasure Hunt Bible Adventure iron-on transfers**—These colorful transfers allow adults and children to create wearable mementos of their treasure hunt.
- **Treasure Hunt Bible Adventure photo frames**—Help kids remember Treasure Hunt Bible Adventure fun. These sturdy 4x6-inch cardboard frames feature the Treasure Hunt Bible Adventure logo and provide plenty of room for you to add your church's name and address. Insert inexpensive photos you've shot during your program, and offer them for sale—or give them to children as special gifts they'll treasure all summer!
- **Treasure Hunt Bible Adventure photo backdrop poster**—Create extra-special photos with this full-color, oversize Treasure Hunt Bible Adventure backdrop. Hang the backdrop on a wall or have volunteers hold it up. Kids can step right up as your photographer snaps their pictures.
- **Chadder Chipmunk items**—Chadder is now available in two sizes: large plush puppet, and adult-size costume pattern (for any adult "chipmunk-wannabe!"). Preschoolers will love having Chadder visit their room. The Preschool Bible Treasure Land Director Manual suggests ways to make this furry friend part of your Treasure Hunt Bible Adventure program. You can give Chadder puppets to volunteers to thank them for their help or you can use Chadder puppets to reinforce Bible learning at other children's ministry events.

A CLUE FOR YOU!

To make your photo frames extra special, affix a magnetic strip to the back of the frame. (For extra ease, use magnetic strips that have adhesive on one side.) Children can hang the pictures on their refrigerator doors for a constant reminder of VBS fun!

Taking Home THE TREASURE

Why Are Family Resources So Important?

Your Treasure Hunt Bible Adventure will reach a variety of children from countless backgrounds. Each of these children (and their families) can benefit from having Treasure Hunt Bible Adventure resources at home. Not only do the following family resources remind kids of Treasure Hunt Bible Adventure fun, but they also provide excellent Bible reinforcement for months after your program has ended. A *Treasure Hunt Sing & Play* audiocassette may be the only Christian music heard in some children's homes.

Field Test Findings

"My child hasn't stopped singing those Treasure Hunt Bible Adventure songs!" We hear this so often, and—we admit—we smile every time! It's great to know that kids are singing phrases such as "I stand alone on the Word of God" or "Hey now, I'm gonna pray for you." That's why we believe it's so important to get these resources into homes everywhere.

CLUES FOR YOU!

Field Test Findings

It never fails...each year at our field test, we always sell out of the Sing & Play audiocassettes! This year, at least 25 percent of the families that attended VBS took home a Sing & Play audiocassette. Even if you offer the cassettes at a minimal price, you can use this outreach as a fund-raiser for VBS or other children's ministry programs. This music is a dynamite way to get God's Word into homes!

"Selling things at church? That seems so commercial!" We've heard this cry before, but experience has shown that providing these quality, kid-friendly resources is an excellent way to reinforce Bible learning at home. When kids listen to Treasure Hunt Sing & Play songs, they're reminded of the treasure of Jesus. Each time kids look at their rain forest photos, they'll be reminded of the fun they had exploring God's Word. And kids can even use *Chadder's Treasure Hunt Adventure* video to share the good news of Jesus with their friends! It works!

What Are Family Resources?

In the Starter Kit, you'll find an order form that lists 5 family resources that reinforce Bible learning. From our field tests, we know that kids love items such as the *Treasure Hunt Sing & Play* audiocassette and CD and *Chadder's Treasure Hunt Adventure* videotape. In fact, several parents arrived early on Day 5 so they could be sure to purchase the limited number of cassettes we had!

Kids love to have mementos of their time at Treasure Hunt Bible Adventure. Items such as Chadder plush puppets, Treasure Hunt Bible Adventure T-shirts, and iron-on transfers are great reminders of your program.

How Can Families Get These Resources?

We realize you're busy; after all, you've just coordinated a VBS program! So we've made it simple to get these important items into the hands of the kids in your program. In the Starter Kit, you'll find an order form for 5 family resources. Now you have three options:

Option 1: Individual Orders

Distribute the order form at the end of Treasure Hunt Sing & Play on Day 5. Let kids know that they can order the Treasure Hunt Sing & Play music, Chadder videos, and other fun stuff simply by taking the order form to their local Christian bookstore. Then send the forms home, and let kids and their families act from there.

Option 2: One Church Order

Distribute the order form at the end of Treasure Hunt Sing & Play on Day 5. Let kids know that they can order the Treasure Hunt Sing & Play music, Chadder videos, and other fun stuff by having a parent help them fill out the order form. Tell kids they'll then need to bring their money and order form (in an envelope) to you by a specified date. You'll probably want to put the date in your church bulletin the following Sunday.

After the due date, tally the total number of each item, and fill it in on a blank order form or a photocopy of the form on page 162 of this manual. Be sure to keep the original order forms so you can distribute items accurately! Take the master order form to your local Christian bookstore, and purchase the items. The next Sunday, set up a table to distribute Treasure Hunt Bible Adventure materials.

Option 3: Rain Forest Marketplace

Make it extra easy for families to take home VBS fun, by setting up a Rain Forest Marketplace! Use the order form to order items a few weeks before your Treasure Hunt Bible Adventure begins. (Check out the box on page 161 to help determine quantities.) Then set a price for each item. Decide how much money you'll earn on

each item you sell. Remember—any money you make can go to your church's missions, children's ministry program, or to local community outreach programs.

Then set up shop! Place the items on a table, just outside the Treasure Time Finale area. Staff your Rain Forest Marketplace with a few willing volunteers (or youth group members) and open your "doors" after Treasure Time Finale ends. You'll be amazed at the overwhelming response!

RECOMMENDED ADVANCE ORDER QUANTITIES

Item	Quantity
Chadder's Treasure Hunt Adventure video	10 percent of VBS enrollment
Treasure Hunt Sing & Play audiocassette	20 percent of VBS enrollment
Chadder plush puppet (small)	5 percent of VBS enrollment
Rain Forest photo frame	75 percent of VBS enrollment

It's that easy!

Field Test Findings

In all of our field test experience, we've found that families really wanted to purchase mementos of a spectacular, meaningful week. You'll be amazed at the overwhelming response when you make these items available.

STUDENT ORDER FORM

Name _____

Address _____

_____

City _____ State _____ ZIP _____

Phone _____

Complete this order form and return it to your **VBS director.** Or inquire at your local Christian bookstore for these great *Treasure Hunt Bible Adventure* items!

HOW MANY	TITLE	ITEM NO.	PRICE	TOTAL COST
	1. *Treasure Hunt Sing & Play* audiocassette	#646847-99034-2	$10.99	
	2. *Treasure Hunt Sing & Play Music & Clip Art CD*	#646847-99042-7	$14.99	
	3. *Chadder's Treasure Hunt Adventure* video	#646847-99003-8	$19.99	
	4. Treasure Hunt Bible Adventure T-Shirt (Adult XL)	#646847-10025-3	$14.99	
	5. Chadder Plush Puppet	#646847-09056-1	$35.99	

Subtotal $ _____

Shipping & Handling $ _____

Sales tax (CA 7.25%, CO 3%, GA 4%, IA 5%, OH 5%) $ _____

TOTAL $ _____

You can also mail this completed order form and payment to:
Group Publishing, Inc., P.O. Box 485, Loveland, CO 80539

PLEASE ADD SHIPPING AND HANDLING FROM THE CHART BELOW.

SHIPPING & HANDLING

ORDER SUBTOTAL	SHIPPING & HANDLING
Up to $12	$3.50
$12.01-$20.00	$4.90
$20.01-$50.00	$5.90
$50.01-$75.00	$7.90
$75.01-$100.00	$11.90
$100.01-$150.00	$15.90
$150.01-$200.00	$19.90
$200.01+	$24.90

CLUES FOR YOU!

Health and SAFETY CONCERNS

Each Discovery Site leader manual gives safety tips for specific Discovery Site activities. As Treasure Hunt Director, however, you're responsible for larger health and safety concerns that may affect the entire VBS. The information below may alert you to health and safety concerns that require your attention.

Health Issues

You'll want to maintain a first-aid kit in a central location. Stock your first-aid kit with adhesive bandages of different sizes, first-aid cream, antibacterial ointment, sterile gauze pads, and insect repellent. You may also want to provide a place for children to lie down if they feel ill. Keep children's registration forms near your first-aid area so you can call parents or caregivers in case of serious injury.

Your Treasure Hunt Bible Adventure registration form provides a spot for parents or caregivers to identify food allergies. Dairy allergies are common, but you may also have children who are allergic to gluten (wheat, rye, barley, or oats); nuts; or other foods.

Most of the snacks suggested in the Treasure Treats Leader Manual will require only slight modifications for children with food allergies. Consult with the Treasure Treats Leader about modifying snacks or about substituting flavored rice cakes, popcorn, fruits, or raw vegetables to accommodate children with food allergies.

Insurance: Make Sure You're Covered

Your church probably already has an insurance policy or policies that are intended to protect you from loss as a result of fire, theft, injury, or lawsuits. Your program is probably covered by your regular insurance, but you should double-check with your insurance agent to be sure. You're not likely to have serious injuries, but you'll want to be prepared just in case.

Facilities: Keeping Your Rain Forest Beautiful

Many accidents can be prevented by well-maintained facilities. After you've selected Discovery Site meeting areas, check each area for potential hazards.

Remove broken or dangerous items, and be sure to lock storage areas that contain chemicals, cleaning solutions, or other toxic materials.

Your church is about to become a high-traffic area! Keep in mind that you'll probably need to clean bathrooms and empty trash daily. You'll also want to spot-check hallways, lobbies, and meeting rooms for trash, stray Clue Crew treasure bags, and lost-and-found items.

Child Abuse: Keeping Kids Safe

Child abuse can take many forms. While you may feel sure that no one in your church would physically or sexually abuse a child in your program, emotional abuse or neglect can be harder to detect. Prevent child abuse by enlisting only staff members that you know and trust and by discussing your concerns and expectations with them ahead of time.

Treasure Hunt Bible Adventure field test directors reported few or no discipline problems. But you'll want to talk with your staff about how you'll handle any that do arise. Discuss appropriate and inappropriate staff responses to situations that require discipline. Photocopy and distribute the "What's a Clue Crew Leader?" handout from page 113 of this manual. This handout suggests positive-language responses for easy classroom management. Remind staff members that you expect them to model God's love in all they say and do.

Treasure Hunt Bible Adventure activities are designed so that children are always supervised by a Discovery Site Leader and several Clue Crew Leaders. You may want to point this out to parents who are concerned about adequate supervision. To avoid even the appearance of impropriety, encourage each staff member to avoid spending time alone with a child. Suggest that staff members escort children in pairs or small groups for bathroom and drinking fountain stops.

Use these health and safety tips to set up a Treasure Hunt Bible Adventure program that ensures the physical, emotional, and spiritual well-being of everyone involved.

A CLUE FOR YOU!

Some churches require volunteers to go through a short class, seminar, or workshop on appropriate actions when working with children. This is an excellent idea, especially if less-experienced teenagers and adults will be helping out. Check with your church leaders to see if they know of (or have led) a class that would be helpful to you.

Kids With SPECIAL NEEDS

Physical Disabilities

If you know you'll have physically challenged children at your program, you'll need to make sure your Discovery Site areas are wheelchair accessible. You may also want to recruit a staff member to look out for these children. This staff member can ask parents or caretakers about specific needs such as
- whether kids have special equipment such as wheelchairs,
- what kids can and cannot eat,
- what kids need help doing,
- what kids like to do for themselves, and
- what kids enjoy most.

Because children work together and help each other in Clue Crews, most physically challenged children will get the help they need from their crew members and Clue Crew Leaders. However, if a physically challenged child needs constant help to participate in Discovery Site activities, consider assigning an additional Clue Crew Leader to his or her crew. For this position, choose someone who will be sensitive and who is capable of responding to the child's needs.

Physically challenged children may be shy, but often they're very bright and innovative. Clue Crew Leaders can encourage them to shine in Discovery Sites that include group discussion, such as Chadder's Treasure Hunt Theater or Bible Exploration. (Plus, as kids carry out their crew roles, they'll all discover how important each crew member is!)

Learning Disabilities

Educators estimate that up to 20 percent of today's children have some type of learning disability. That means that in a program of one hundred children, up to twenty kids could be battling with dyslexia, attention-deficit/hyperactivity disorder, or other learning disabilities. Kids with learning disabilities aren't lazy or dumb—they just learn differently than other children do.

Treasure Hunt Bible Adventure works for children with learning disabilities! Here's why:

- **It doesn't rely heavily on reading skills.** Children who enjoy reading can volunteer to be Readers for their Clue Crews. Children who have trouble

Field Test Findings

Everyone *can* do the activities at Treasure Hunt Bible Adventure! A physically challenged boy attended our field test, and he jumped right in and tried it all. Some activities were more challenging, but with the help of his crew members and a little flexibility, he was able to participate fully in every activity. What a wonderful reminder that we're all treasures to Jesus!

reading can choose other equally important jobs.

● **It allows kids processing time.** Because each Clue Crew has a Clue Crew Leader, Discovery Site Leaders don't have to single out kids who need special help. Crew leaders can help the kids in their Clue Crews work at their own pace. And Discovery Site Leaders are free to go around and check in with children as they complete their activities.

● **It doesn't require children to think sequentially.** Fifty percent of all students are frustrated by sequential-type assignments. At Treasure Hunt Bible Adventure, children don't have to master a new set of information each day. Instead, they learn one basic Point that's reinforced in different ways for different kinds of learners.

If you know or suspect that kids with learning disabilities will be attending your program, let your leaders know. Encourage them to help these children by
- giving instructions one at a time,
- using the positive-language suggestions in the "What's a Clue Crew Leader?" handout (p. 113),
- ignoring harmless annoying behaviors, and
- praising children sincerely and often.

For more information on attention-deficit/hyperactivity disorder (ADHD), use the address below to contact Children and Adults with Attention Deficit Disorders.

Children and Adults with Attention Deficit Disorders
499 N.W. 70th Ave. #101
Plantation, FL 33317
(954) 587-3700

Welcoming NEWCOMERS

Summer is a busy time for families. Some kids may come to Treasure Hunt Bible Adventure all five days; some may come for two or three days and then drop out; others may join your Treasure Hunt Bible Adventure program midcourse. Use the following ideas to welcome newcomers to your adventure.

● **Start with small Clue Crews.** When you assign kids to Clue Crews, limit some crews to three or four kids instead of five. If new kids join your program, you can assign them to Clue Crews in which you've left openings. Even if you don't have many visitors, kids in smaller crews will love the additional attention they'll get from their Clue Crew Leaders. If you want to encourage visitors to

attend, challenge kids to fill their crews by inviting their friends!

● **Have kids introduce new Clue Crew members.** Instead of escorting a visitor to a Clue Crew yourself, invite one of the crew members to do it. Recruit an outgoing member of the visitor's assigned crew (a Cheerleader may be a good candidate for this job), and then introduce the visitor to the other child one on one. Help the child describe the Clue Crew, including the crew name, the crew jobs, and the daily schedule. Then send the pair of children back to meet the rest of the crew.

● **Cheer for visitors each day during Treasure Hunt Sing & Play.** Have the Treasure Hunt Sing & Play Leader invite Clue Crews to stand if they have new members. Have Cheerleaders introduce their new crew members; then have the Treasure Hunt Sing & Play Leader lead everyone in shouting, "Welcome!"

Responsibility: LET 'EM HAVE IT!

At Treasure Hunt Bible Adventure, Discovery Site Leaders provide fun, hands-on, Bible-learning activities. Clue Crew Leaders shepherd and guide their Clue Crews. But kids take responsibility for their own learning.

Even the most well-intentioned Discovery Site Leaders and Clue Crew Leaders may be uncomfortable giving kids this much responsibility. After all, they're the leaders; they've prepared the material, and they know what kids should learn. Treasure Treats Leaders may insist that it's easier to prepare snacks ahead of time instead of counting on kids to complete the work. Clue Crew Leaders may be tempted to complete Craft Cave projects for kids instead of helping them complete their own.

Every activity at your Treasure Hunt Bible Adventure program has been field-tested, revised, retested, and revised again. So you can have confidence that kids will be able to follow directions and complete the activities successfully within the allotted times. Instead of doing kids' work for them, leaders should encourage Clue Crew members to help kids discover Jesus by helping each other complete activities.

By the end of the week, you'll hear reports of kids leading their own discussions, helping each other complete projects, and cheering each other on. Trust the Lord, and trust your kids—and watch God's love surround your program!

ENDING THE EXPEDITION

Closing Program and FOLLOW-UP IDEAS

FOLLOW-UP IDEAS

Helping Children KNOW JESUS

At Treasure Hunt Bible Adventure, children don't just hear about God's love—they see it, touch it, sing it, taste it, and put it into action. As they travel from Discovery Site to Discovery Site, they discover that the Bible is the map and Jesus is the treasure. Most importantly, children learn that God sent his Son, Jesus, to die for our sins because he loves us.

You'll notice that there's no "set" time for children to make a faith commitment. We feel that Treasure Hunt Bible Adventure helps children build relationships—with other children, adults, and with Jesus. And since each child is at a different point in his or her relationship with Jesus, programming a time for commitment may be confusing to some children. However, if it's part of your church tradition to include a time for children to make a faith decision, feel free to add it in during the Treasure Time Finale on Day 4.

Some children may want to know more about making Jesus part of their lives. If you sense that a child might like to know more about what it means to follow Jesus, give this simple explanation:

God loves us so much that he sent his Son, Jesus, to die on the cross for us. Jesus died and rose again so we could be forgiven for all the wrong things we do. Jesus wants to be our forever friend. If we ask him to, he'll take away the wrong things we've done and fill our lives with his love. As our forever friend, Jesus will always be with us and will help us make the right choices. And if we believe in Jesus, someday we'll live with him forever in heaven.

You may want to lead the child in a simple prayer inviting Jesus to be his or her forever friend. You may also want to share one or more of the following Scripture passages with the child. Encourage the child to read the Scripture passages with you from his or her own Bible.

- John 3:16
- Romans 5:8-11
- Romans 6:23
- Ephesians 2:5-8

Be sure to share the news of the child's spiritual development with his or her parent(s).

Permission to photocopy this explanation from Group's Treasure Hunt Bible Adventure: Treasure Hunt Bible Adventure Director Manual granted for local church use. Copyright © Group Publishing, Inc., P.O. Box 481, Loveland, CO 80539.

You've Found THE TREASURE!

Thanks for joining us at Group's Treasure Hunt Bible Adventure! Now that you've found the treasure, you can sit back, relax, and congratulate yourself and your staff on a job well done. Then thank God for his blessings on your program. In this section, you'll find ideas that will help you to wrap up your program and follow up with children and their families. You'll also find helpful evaluation forms you can use to get specific feedback from Discovery Site Leaders and Clue Crew Leaders.

Closing Program: TAKING THE TREASURE HOME

If you want an easy way to give parents and church members a glimpse of your Treasure Hunt Bible Adventure fun, invite them to attend Treasure Time Finale. This fun-filled, Bible-learning time is already built in to your Treasure Hunt Bible Adventure program each day. Explain that parents can join the fun by arriving just twenty minutes early when they come to pick up their children. They'll see children singing Treasure Hunt Sing & Play songs, telling about their daily missions, and actively reviewing the daily Bible story. Parents will really catch the Treasure Hunt Bible Adventure spirit as children celebrate God's love with colorful signs, costumes, and cheers on Day 5.

If you want to have a separate closing program, follow the steps below to set up a Discovery Site "open house." Set up your open house in the evening or even on Sunday morning. Parents and kids will love it!

1. Have Discovery Site Leaders set up the following activities in their respective Discovery Site areas. If you purchased additional *Treasure Hunt Sing & Play* audiocassettes, encourage Discovery Site Leaders to play the

Treasure Hunt Bible Adventure songs while people are visiting their areas.

Treasure Hunt Sing & Play—Have the Treasure Hunt Sing & Play Leader teach words and motions to all thirteen songs (or as many as time allows).

Preschool Bible Treasure Land—Have the Preschool Bible Treasure Land Director set up five or six Jungle Gym Playtime Activities children can visit with their parents. Choose from the activities suggested below, or let the Preschool Director suggest kids' favorites!
- Riverboat Rides (Day 1)
- Tomb Tunnel (Day 4)
- Ping-Pong Puff (Day 5)

Craft Cave—Have the Craft Cave Leader display his or her sample Craft Cave projects (or have kids display the crafts they made—if they're willing to part with them for a little while). Ask the crafts leader to explain the stories of Miguela, Alejo, and Palomita on the "Operation Kid-to-Kid" posters. Have the crafts leader encourage kids to show their parents the surprise of the Surprise Treasure Chests.

Jungle Gym Games—Have the games leader lead families in the Swamp Squish game kids played on Day 1 or Pass-Along Peter (also from Day 1). Families will also enjoy the "Jungle Gym Gems," such as the Backward Waterfall or the Cave of Wonders!

Treasure Treats—Have the Treasure Treats Leader set out supplies for making Prayer Treasure Mix (Day 3). Display a sample snack, and let children and parents make their own tasty treats.

Chadder's Treasure Hunt Theater—Have the Chadder's Treasure Hunt Theater Leader play the *Chadder's Treasure Hunt Adventure* video. Set out paper, markers, and pencils, and let families write letters of advice to Chadder or draw pictures of him. Or, kids can use the extra Bible story stickers (on their Treasure Hunt sticker sheets) to mark where the Bible stories are in their Bibles.

Bible Exploration—Have the Bible Exploration Leader set up the prison ship (Day 5) and take groups inside the ship to hear the story of Paul. (You may even ask Habib to make a surprise appearance!) Parents can become prisoners with their children, and help throw the "grain" overboard. You may want to provide a Student Book for each family to continue searching for the treasures in God's Word.

Treasure Time Finale—Have the Treasure Time Finale Leader lead people in the show from Day 4. Let parents add their paper scraps to the bag, and then watch the "sins" disappear. Have families join together to sing "Oh How I Love Jesus" and talk about how Jesus is the greatest treasure in their lives.

2. Begin by having everyone gather in the sanctuary or the fellowship hall for a brief introduction and a Treasure Hunt Sing & Play time. Have your Treasure Hunt Sing & Play Leader teach everyone "I've Found Me a Treasure." This is a great time to distribute Treasure Hunt Bible Adventure

completion certificates. Simply photocopy the certificates on pages 176 and 177 (or purchase the "You're a Gem!" certificates); fill in children's, Clue Crew Leaders', or Discovery Site Leaders' names; then sign and date each certificate.

3. Designate a thirty- to forty-five-minute time frame in which families can visit the Discovery Sites. At the end of the designated time, use a bamboo whistle to call everyone back to your original meeting area for Treasure Time Finale.

4. Thank everyone for coming, and encourage them to join you in planning and preparing for next year's program.

Your Treasure Hunt Bible Adventure has ended. But helping kids discover Jesus never ends—you still have lots of time to share the good news about Jesus with the kids in your church and community. The outreach efforts you make will help you share God's love with your Treasure Hunt Bible Adventure participants and their families. Use the ideas below to design a follow-up plan that fits your church's needs.

● **Send Treasure Hunt Bible Adventure follow-up postcards.** Kids love getting mail, so here's a sure-fire way to get kids back for Sunday school—a personal invitation from Treasure Hunt Bible Adventure. These colorful postcards help you make a long-term impact on kids by involving them in your regular Sunday school program. *Order these postcards from Group Publishing or your local Christian bookstore.*

● **Give away Treasure Hunt Bible Adventure photos.** Deliver framed photos to families of children who don't regularly attend your church. Kids will treasure these colorful, fun mementos—and you'll have an opportunity to invite the family to visit your church. *Order Treasure Hunt Bible Adventure photo frames from Group Publishing or your local Christian bookstore.*

● **Invite Chadder Chipmunk to visit a children's ministry event.** Schedule a return engagement of *Chadder's Treasure Hunt Adventure* during another children's ministry event. Children who visited your church during Treasure Hunt Bible Adventure will want to come back and revisit their furry friend. Add a live appearance from a Chadder plush puppet, and you'll be sure to fill every

chair! *Order Chadder plush puppets, costume patterns, and* Chadder's Treasure Hunt Adventure *videocassettes from Group Publishing or your local Christian bookstore.*

● **Sponsor a parents day.** Build relationships with children's parents by having a parents day during Treasure Hunt Bible Adventure. Encourage children to invite their parents or older siblings to join them. Provide adult and youth Bible studies or have family members visit the Discovery Sites with their children's Clue Crews. Also require parents to come inside to pick up their children so you can make contact with them.

● **Hold a Treasure Hunt memory night.** Invite all the Treasure Hunt Bible Adventure participants to a get-together every month or every quarter. Make each memory night a fun event that fits the Treasure Hunt Bible Adventure theme. For example, set out paper plates, colored construction paper, yarn, and markers, and allow kids to make wild rain forest animal masks! You'll want to include yummy Treasure Treats at each memory night!

YOU'RE A GEM!

Thanks for
Helping Kids Discover Jesus at

TREASURE HUNT Bible Adventure

You've been a valuable _____ Leader.

_____
Treasure Hunt Bible Adventure Director

_____
Date

FOLLOW-UP IDEAS

Permission to photocopy this certificate from Group's Treasure Hunt Bible Adventure: Treasure Hunt Bible Adventure Director Manual granted for local church use. Copyright © Group Publishing, Inc., P.O. Box 481, Loveland, CO 80539.

Evaluating Your TREASURE HUNT BIBLE ADVENTURE Program

After Treasure Hunt Bible Adventure, you'll want to check in with your Discovery Site Leaders, Clue Crew Leaders, and other staff members to see how things went.

Photocopy the "Discovery Site Leader VBS Evaluation" (p. 180) and the "Clue Crew Leader VBS Evaluation" (p. 181), and distribute the photocopies to your staff. To help your evaluation process go smoothly, you may want to ask staff members to return their evaluations within two weeks of Treasure Hunt Bible Adventure. After two weeks, specific details will still be fresh in staff members' minds, and they'll have a good perspective on their overall experiences.

After you've collected Discovery Site Leader and Clue Crew Leader evaluation forms, please take a few moments to fill out the "Treasure Hunt Bible Adventure Evaluation" on pages 183-184. Be sure to summarize the comments you received from Discovery Site Leaders and Clue Crew Leaders. Keep a copy of your completed evaluation for your records; then return the original to Group's VBS Coordinator. Your detailed feedback will help us meet your needs as we plan an all-new program for next year.

Thanks for choosing Group's Treasure Hunt Bible Adventure!

A CLUE FOR YOU!

You can customize the evaluation forms by adding additional questions in the "Other comments about our Treasure Hunt Bible Adventure program" section. For example, you may want to ask about facilities or about the dates and times of your VBS. This is also a good time to recruit volunteers for next year's VBS. Discovery Site Leaders and Clue Crew Leaders will have had so much fun that they'll want to sign on again!

Discovery Site Leader
VBS EVALUATION

Thanks for joining us at Treasure Hunt Bible Adventure! Please complete this evaluation form to help us plan for next year's VBS.

1. I led the _____ Discovery Site.

2. I spent _____ minutes preparing materials for each day.

3. Were the instructions in your Discovery Site leader manual clear and easy to follow? Explain.

4. What did you like best about your Discovery Site? What did kids like best?

5. What would you like to change about your Discovery Site?

Other comments about our Treasure Hunt Bible Adventure program:

Clue Crew Leader
VBS EVALUATION

Thanks for joining us at Treasure Hunt Bible Adventure! Please complete this evaluation form to help us plan for next year's VBS.

1. What was the best thing about working with your Clue Crew?

2. What was the hardest thing?

3. Did the "For Clue Crew Leaders Only" handouts help you as you worked with kids? Explain.

4. What other training helps or resources would have helped you in your Clue Crew Leader role?

TREASURE HUNT BIBLE ADVENTURE EVALUATION

Thanks for exploring with us!

Will you help us make next year's VBS even better? Take a few moments at the end of your program to fill out this survey. Drop it in the mail, and let us know what you think!

Thank you!

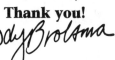

Jody Brolsma
Treasure Hunt Bible Adventure Coordinator

1. What was the number one reason you chose Group's Treasure Hunt Bible Adventure?

2. Tell us how you learned about Group's Treasure Hunt Bible Adventure.
○ Bookstore   ○ Mailing   ○ Advertisement   ○ Other (please specify)

3. Where did you purchase your VBS items?
○ Bookstore   ○ Direct from Group
Why?

4. Tell us how you liked the Treasure Hunt Bible Adventure program.
○ I loved it! I can't wait to see next year's!   ○ It was OK—it met my VBS needs.
○ It didn't work at all for my church.
What, if anything, would you like us to change or improve?

Would you consider using a Group VBS program next summer?
○ Absolutely—here's why...   ○ Maybe—here's why...   ○ No way—here's why...

5. Tell us what was most difficult for you in putting together Treasure Hunt Bible Adventure.

What could we do to make your job easier?

6. Tell us what you liked most about the Treasure Hunt Bible Adventure Director Manual.

What would you change about the Treasure Hunt Bible Adventure Director Manual?

7. Tell us about the music at your VBS.
Which of the following did you use in your Treasure Hunt Sing & Play sessions?
○ *Treasure Hunt Sing & Play Leader Training* video   ○ *Treasure Hunt Sing & Play Transparencies*
○ *Treasure Hunt Sing & Play* audiocassette   ○ piano or guitar accompaniment
○ *Treasure Hunt Sing & Play Music & Clip Art CD*
What, if anything, would you like us to change or improve about VBS music?

Did you use the clip art on the CD?

8. Tell us about your Discovery Sites.
Were your Discovery Sites easy to set up and lead?

What could we do to make it easier for Discovery Site Leaders to do their jobs?

Summarize comments from your Discovery Site Leaders:

9. How did kids respond to Chadder? Would they rather see a new character next year?

10. Tell us about the Bible content of the Treasure Hunt Bible Adventure program.
- ○ There wasn't enough.   ○ It was just right.   ○ There was too much.

11. Tell us about Operation Kid-to-Kid.
Did you do Operation Kid-to-Kid?

What did you like about the mission project?

Would you like to see a mission incorporated each year?

12. We're always looking for fun and innovative themes for our VBS programs. What new ideas would your kids like to see in the future?

13. Would you recommend Group's VBS to a friend?
- ○ Yes, because...
- ○ No, because...

14. For you, what is the best thing about Group's VBS?

If you said something nice about Group's VBS, may we quote you?   ○ Yes

Permission to photocopy this evaluation form from Group's Treasure Hunt Bible Adventure: Treasure Hunt Bible Adventure Director Manual granted for local church use. Copyright © Group Publishing, Inc., P.O. Box 481, Loveland, CO 80539.

Please fold on dotted lines with the below flap facing outside and tape closed. Thank you.

NAME _____
ADDRESS _____
CITY _____ STATE _____ ZIP _____

BUSINESS REPLY MAIL
FIRST-CLASS MAIL   PERMIT NO 16   LOVELAND CO

POSTAGE WILL BE PAID BY ADDRESSEE

VBS COORDINATOR
P.O. BOX 481
LOVELAND, CO 80539-9985

NO POSTAGE
NECESSARY
IF MAILED
IN THE
UNITED STATES

INDEX

accompanist (see MUSIC ACCOMPANIST)
announcements 51
attention-deficit/hyperactivity disorder (ADHD) 166
attention-getting device (see BAMBOO WHISTLE)
backup plans 49
bamboo whistle 106, 158
Bible distribution 36
Bible Exploration
 (Discovery Site where kids hear the day's Bible story
 and reflect upon its implications in their lives) 11, 17, 21, 28, 46, 60
Bible Exploration Leader 89
Bible partners 37
Bible Points 10, 20
Bible stories 10, 20
Bible verses 10, 20
budget 43
bulletin inserts 48, 49, 121, 125
calendar (see PLANNING CALENDAR)
certificates (see COMPLETION CERTIFICATES)
Chadder Chipmunk
 (chipmunk puppet who is the main character
 in the *Chadder's Treasure Hunt Adventure* video) 30
Chadder Chipmunk costume pattern 122
Chadder Chipmunk plush puppet 122
***Chadder's Treasure Hunt Adventure* video**
 (video that is shown during Chadder's Treasure
 Hunt Theater and that stars Chadder Chipmunk) 17, 30, 44
Chadder's Treasure Hunt Theater
 (Discovery Site where kids watch a video
 that shows them how the day's Bible Point
 relates to their lives) 11, 17, 21, 30, 45, 64
Chadder's Treasure Hunt Theater Leader 90
child abuse 164
child-care coordinator 99
choir (see TREASURE HUNT SING & PLAY)

clip art 121, 124
closing program 172
Clue Crew assignments 49, 72, 137
Clue Crew jobs 18, 26, 115
Clue Crew Leaders, job descriptions (see JOB DESCRIPTIONS)
Clue Crew Leaders
  (teens or adults who supervise
  Clue Crews as they travel to
  Discovery Sites) 18, 24, 28, 44, 46, 48, 50, 52, 93, 94, 95, 96, 107, 113, 144
Clue Crews
  (combined-age groups, each of five
  children and one Clue Crew Leader
  who travel together to Discovery Sites
  and participate as a team in various activities) 18, 23, 25, 72
Clue Crews, combined-age 25, 49, 51, 138
Clue Crew treasure bags 26, 138
combined-age Clue Crews (see CLUE CREWS, COMBINED-AGE)
community fliers (see FLIERS)
completion certificates 51, 53, 176, 177
Craft Cave
  (Discovery Site where kids make action
  crafts and Operation Kid-to-Kid Magnetic Bookmarks) 10, 17, 21, 45, 61
Craft Cave Leader 86
crafts (see CRAFT CAVE)
daily points (see BIBLE POINTS)
daily schedules 47, 72
decorating 50, 52, 56
devotions 153
director (see TREASURE HUNT DIRECTOR)
disabled kids (see SPECIAL-NEEDS KIDS)
discipline 49, 51
***Discover!* video**
  (video that gives a brief overview
  of the Treasure Hunt Bible Adventure and
  provides training for staff) 12, 46, 47, 49, 103, 122
Discovery Site leader manuals 12
Discovery Site Leaders
  (adults or mature teenagers
  who lead Discovery Sites) 18, 44, 72, 83, 84, 107, 144
Discovery Site Leaders, job descriptions (see JOB DESCRIPTIONS)
Discovery Sites
  (learning areas where children engage
  in specific activities such as crafts, games,
  songs, or learning the Bible story) 10-11, 17, 22-23, 58, 72

Discovery Site Sign-In
  (registration and entrance area for
  Treasure Hunt Bible Adventure) 56
Discovery Site Sign-In personnel 56
dyslexia 165
Elementary Student Books (see STUDENT BOOKS)
emergency plans 49, 112
evaluations 53, 179
facilities 45, 56, 163
faith commitment 171
faith decision 171
families 55, 159, 175
family resource coordinator 99
first aid (see HEALTH AND SAFETY)
fliers 48, 121, 129
follow-up ideas 174
food allergies 163
games (see JUNGLE GYM GAMES)
groups 72
health and safety 51, 163
helping children follow Jesus 171
insurance 163
intergenerational programs 55
International Bible Society 35, 36
invitation to parents 121, 127
job descriptions 83, 85, 94, 95, 96
Jungle Gym Games
  (Discovery Site where kids
  enjoy recreational activities) 10, 17, 21, 45, 64
Jungle Gym Games Leader 87
Kid-to-Kid Send-Off Center 36, 38
leader training 46, 48, 101
leaders (see DISCOVERY SITE LEADERS)
learning disabled kids (see SPECIAL-NEEDS KIDS)
learning types 17
locations (see SETTINGS)
memory verses 19
middle schoolers 27
music accompanist 100
newcomers 166
news release 39, 48, 121, 128
open house 172
Operation Kid-to-Kid
  (missions project kids participate
  in to learn they can impact the world) 35

187

Operation Kid-to-Kid packet 38
"Operation Kid-to-Kid" posters 36, 173
Operation Kid-to-Kid update 38
Operation Kid-to-Kid Web site 38
order form 160-162
outreach 24, 50, 52, 138, 174
overview (see TREASURE HUNT BIBLE ADVENTURE OVERVIEW)
parent letter (see INVITATION TO PARENTS)
Photographer 98
physically disabled kids (see SPECIAL-NEEDS KIDS)
planning calendar 43
posters (also see "OPERATION KID-TO-KID" POSTERS)
preregistration 47, 48, 135
Preschool Bible Treasure Land
   (area where preschoolers enjoy
   age-appropriate activities) 22, 46, 66, 72, 118
Preschool Bible Treasure Land **audiocassette** 158
Preschool Bible Treasure Land Director Manual 12
Preschool Bible Treasure Land Director 92
Preschool Bible Treasure Land overview 9
Preschool Student Books (see STUDENT BOOKS)
publicity coordinator 99
publicity skit 49, 130
publicity 44, 47, 48, 119
recreation (see JUNGLE GYM GAMES)
recruiting staff 44, 46, 47, 83, 93, 99
Registrar 97, 141
registration workers 100
registration 28, 50, 133, 143
resources 158-162
   (also see ORDER FORM)
responsibility 18, 167
safety concerns (see HEALTH AND SAFETY)
schedules (see DAILY SCHEDULES)
settings 54, 55
singing (see TREASURE HUNT SING & PLAY)
skit (see PUBLICITY SKIT)
slide show 53, 98
snacks (see TREASURE TREATS)
songs (see TREASURE HUNT SING & PLAY)
Spanish translations of the Gospel of John 29, 35
special-needs kids 49, 165
spiritual development 171
Starter Kit 12, 44
stickers (see TREASURE HUNT STICKER SHEETS)

Student Books
  (for elementary children, the Gospel
  of John; for preschool children, an age-
  appropriate Bible story book with activity
  sheets and family newsletters) 13, 29, 48
supplies 44, 47, 48, 51, 52, 59, 70, 104, 140, 141
table tent 49, 121, 126
teachers (see DISCOVERY SITE LEADERS)
teenagers 28
training (see LEADER TRAINING)
transportation coordinator 99
Treasure Chest Quest 26, 91
Treasure Hunt Bible Adventure Director Manual 12
Treasure Hunt Bible Adventure Overview
  (chart that describes the Treasure Hunt
  Bible Adventure's activities for the week) 9, 10
Treasure Hunt Director
  (the individual who organizes and oversees
  Treasure Hunt Bible Adventure) 43, 56
Treasure Hunt Sign-In personnel 97
Treasure Hunt Sing & Play
  (first Discovery Site of the day, where
  kids sing songs with motions) 10, 17, 20, 45, 50, 51, 59
Treasure Hunt Sing & Play **audiocassette** 13, 158
Treasure Hunt Sing & Play **Leader** 50, 85
Treasure Hunt Sing & Play **Leader Training video** 104
Treasure Hunt Sing & Play **Music & Clip Art CD** 158
Treasure Hunt Sing & Play **Transparencies** 158
Treasure Hunt sticker sheets 26
Treasure Time Finale
  (last Discovery Site of the day; kids review
  the story and Bible Point of the day
  through drama and other interactive activities) 11, 18, 21, 46, 51, 65
Treasure Time Finale Leader 91
Treasure Treats
  (Discovery Site where kids make and eat snacks) 11, 17, 21, 45, 62
Treasure Treats Leader 31, 88
Treasure Treats Leader Manual 31, 163
Treasure Treats Service 31, 45, 72
T-shirts 158
upper-elementary kids (see MIDDLE SCHOOLERS)
video night 98
visitors (see NEWCOMERS)
volunteers 47, 53, 56, 97, 100, 141, 142, 164, 179
www.OK2K.com (see OPERATION KID-TO-KID WEB SITE)

TEACH YOUR PRESCHOOLERS AS JESUS TAUGHT WITH GROUP'S *HANDS-ON BIBLE CURRICULUM*™

Hands-On Bible Curriculum™ **for preschoolers** helps your preschoolers learn the way they learn best—by touching, exploring, and discovering. With active and authentic learning, preschoolers love learning about the Bible, and they really remember what they learn.

Because small children learn best through repetition, Preschoolers and Pre-K & K will learn one important point per lesson, and Toddlers & 2s will learn one point each month with **Hands-On Bible Curriculum**. These important lessons will stick with them and comfort them during their daily lives. Your children will learn God is our friend, who Jesus is, and we can always trust Jesus.

The **Learning Lab**® is packed with age-appropriate learning tools for fun, faith-building lessons. Toddlers & 2s explore big **Interactive StoryBoards**™ with enticing textures that toddlers love to touch—like sandpaper for earth, cotton for clouds, and blue cellophane for water. While they hear the Bible story, children also *touch* the Bible story. And they learn. **Bible Big Books**™ captivate Preschoolers and Pre-K & K while teaching them important Bible lessons. With **Jumbo Bible Puzzles**™ and involving **Learning Mats**™, your children will see, touch, and explore their Bible stories. Each quarter there's a brand new collection of supplies to keep your lessons fresh and involving.

Just order one **Learning Lab** and one **Teacher Guide** for each age level, add a few common classroom supplies, and presto—you have everything you need to inspire and build faith in your children. For more interactive fun, introduce your children to the age-appropriate puppet (Cuddles the Lamb, Whiskers the Mouse, or Pockets the Kangaroo) who will be your teaching assistant and their friend. No student books are required!

Hands-On Bible Curriculum is also available for elementary grades.

Order today from your local Christian bookstore, or write: Group Publishing, P.O. Box 485, Loveland, CO 80539.

BRING THE BIBLE TO LIFE FOR YOUR 1ST- THROUGH 6TH-GRADERS... WITH GROUP'S HANDS-ON BIBLE CURRICULUM™

Energize your kids with Authentic Learning!

In each lesson, students will participate in exciting and memorable learning experiences using fascinating gadgets and gizmos. Your elementary students will discover biblical truths and <u>remember</u> what they learn because they're <u>doing</u> instead of just listening.

You'll save time and money too!

Simply follow the quick and easy instructions in the **Teacher Guide**. You'll get tons of material for an energy-packed 35- to 60- minute lesson. Plus, you'll SAVE BIG over other curriculum programs that require you to buy expensive separate student books—all student handouts in Group's **Hands-On Bible Curriculum** are photocopiable!

In addition to the easy-to-use **Teacher Guide**, you'll get all the essential teaching materials you need in a ready-to-use **Learning Lab**®. No more running from store to store hunting for lesson materials—all the active-learning tools you need to teach 13 exciting Bible lessons to any size class are provided for you in the **Learning Lab**.

Challenging topics each quarter keep your kids coming back!

Group's **Hands-On Bible Curriculum** covers topics that matter to your kids and teaches them the Bible with integrity. Switching topics every month keeps your 1st- through 6th-graders enthused and coming back for more. The full two-year program will help your kids make God-pleasing decisions...recognize their God-given potential...and seek to grow as Christians.

Take the boredom out of Sunday school, children's church, and midweek meetings for your elementary students. Make your job easier and more rewarding with no-fail lessons that are ready in a flash. Order Group's **Hands-On Bible Curriculum** for your 1st- through 6th-graders today. (Also available for Toddlers & 2s, Preschool, and Pre-K and K!)

Order today from your local Christian bookstore, or write: Group Publishing, P.O. Box 485, Loveland, CO 80539.

Year-Round Fun for Your Children's Ministry

Bible Story Games for Preschoolers

Preschoolers learn by playing, and with these simple, age-appropriate games, children actually learn and *remember* Bible stories! You'll get 100 easy-to-do games that all tie in to Bible stories and use few or no supplies. These "everyone-wins" games help children feel good about church and themselves and give teachers a wide range of games to fit in with any Bible lesson.

ISBN 0-7644-2059-3 $15.99

Bible-Time Crafts Your Kids Will Love

From arks to zithers, each of these 47 crafts has a biblical and historical significance. That means you will use crafts again and again for dozens of Bible stories. Step-by-step directions make crafts easy, Bible background explains how items were used in Bible times, and a wrap-up activity for each craft helps kids use them at home.

ISBN 0-7644-2067-4 $14.99

Children's Church Specials

Here are 15 new, easy-to-lead worship sessions—each built around a specific characteristic of God! Children will learn to know and love God as they participate in upbeat praise, a memory-building activity, and worshipful prayer. As an added benefit, six of the worship services connect to holidays!

ISBN 0-7644-2063-1 $15.99

Strong & Simple Messages for Children's Ministry
Ruth Reazin

Make children's messages easy and memorable with these 53 flexible, quick-prep ways to teach Bible truths! Memorable object lessons drive home important Bible truths for kids—and make life easy for Sunday school teachers and children's workers! Perfect for high-impact children's sermons, lessons, and devotions.

ISBN 0-7644-2051-8 $12.99

Order today from your local Christian bookstore, or write: Group Publishing, P.O. Box 485, Loveland, CO 80539.